UNFETTERED

_____

DORLAN'S PLAN

AMS PRESS
NEW YORK

UNFETTERED.

A NOVEL.

BY

SUTTON E. GRIGGS,

Author of " IMPERIUM IN IMPERIO," "OVERSHADOWED,"
" DORLAN'S PLAN," Etc.

NASHVILLE, TENN.:
THE ORION PUBLISHING COMPANY.
1902.

Reprinted from the edition of 1902, Nashville

First AMS EDITION published 1971

Manufactured in the United States of America

International Standard Book Number: 0-404-00168-8

Library of Congress Catalog Number: 79-144623

AMS PRESS INC.
NEW YORK, N.Y.   10003

DEDICATION.

———

While a last beloved sister

MARY,

Was, with patience and fortitude, awaiting the
slow but certain tread of the Grim Reaper,
she spared strength enough to read, from
beginning to end, "Overshadowed,"
that came to greet her ere she sped
to the home of the departed.
Were she mindful of happenings on the
earth to-day the author of this volume would
be sure of at least one sympathetic reader.
To her memory "Unfettered" is
affectionately dedicated.

THE AUTHOR.

"The chains that bound the body * * were as tender chords of mercy compared with the shackles that gyved his mind * * ."—*Kelley Miller*.

AUTHOR'S PREFACE.

On a sad occasion in days gone by, the people of the United States were called upon to deal with the Negro's woes, and in the haze of battle there arose to thrill the hearts of men a Fort Sumter, a Bull Run, a Gettysburg, and, at last, an Appomattox.

Since those pregnant days, in spite of a seeming retrogression in some quarters, there has been a steady, unbroken march of the Negro in an upward direction. One day our great nation that once dealt with the Negro's woes will be summoned to deal with his strength, to kindly accept or finally reject *all* that he can do.

As the day of final adjustment is inevitable, it is wise for all of us who love our country to make a study of the internal workings of a race now shaking itself loose from the death sleep of the ages.

It is the aim of "UNFETTERED" to lead the reader into the inner life of the Negro race and lay bare the aspirations that are fructifying there.

Those who come to these pages in quest of pen pictures of either angels or demons, are not likely to find what they seek, for our story has to do with human beings, simply. That is, we should say, with the exception of—but you will make your own exceptions when the tale is fully told.

THE AUTHOR.

CONTENTS.

DORLAN'S PLAN.

CHAPTER I.

AN ANGLO-SAXON'S DEATH.

Gently the midsummer breezes rustled the green leaves of the giant oaks and towering poplars that stood guard over the Dalton house, which, as though spurning their protection, rose majestically above them and commanded a splendid view of the Tennessee fields and woodlands, stretching far out on either side of the leisurely flowing Cumberland.

The subdued whisperings of the winds, their elf-like tread as they cautiously crept from tree top to tree top, tended to create the suspicion that they were aware of the tragedy which their mother, Nature, was so soon to enact within the walls of the house around which we now see them hovering.

In a sumptuously furnished room of this magnificent structure, Maurice Dalton, the present owner thereof, lies dying; battling heroically yet losingly in that last, inevitable conflict which he had been summoned to wage with the forces of decay. The head of this dying Anglo-Saxon rests, in these its last moments, on the bosom of Aunt Catherine, an aged Negro woman, who was his

(9)

first and loving nurse in infancy, and has been his one unswerving friend and worshipper in all of his after life.

On former occasions, when disease had drawn him to the edge of the grave, so skillfully did Aunt Catherine second the recuperative work of nature that he was led back to life and health. Now that her healing art has failed her, she sits heartbroken, and, like Rachel weeping for her children, refuses to be comforted. No mother ever loved an offspring with greater intensity than Aunt Catherine loved "Maury," as she called him.

Near to Aunt Catherine stands Lemuel Dalton, a nephew and the sole surviving relative of Maurice Dalton. Tall, slender and well featured, he was an interesting figure at any time. His firm, gray eyes give evidence of great grief over the approaching death of his uncle, although the death of this uncle is his only known means of an early escape from poverty.

At the foot of the bed on which Maurice Dalton lies, stands Morlene, a beautiful girl just budding into womanhood. She is a Negro, although her very pleasing complexion is so light as to give plain evidence of a strong infusion of Anglo-Saxon blood.

A wealth of lovely black hair crowning a head of perfect shape and queenly poise; a face, the subtle charm of which baffles description; two lustrous black eyes, wondrously expressive, presided over by eyebrows that were ideally beautiful; a neck which, with infinite regard for the requirements of perfect art, descended and expanded so as to form part of a faultless bust; as to form, magnificently well proportioned; when viewed as a whole, the very essence of loveliness. Such was the picture of Morlene, who, once seen, left an image that never again passed from the mind of the beholder.

Morlene's bosom is just now the abode of many surging emotions. She views in a dying and speechless state the person who alone on earth knows the secret of her parentage. Maurice Dalton had promised to impart this information to Morlene at some time, but has delayed doing so until now it appears to be too late. Add to the fact that Maurice Dalton is carrying to the silence of the grave the information so earnestly, passionately desired by Morlene, the further fact that he had been her support, protection, and sole dependence from earliest infancy. So keen had been his interest in Morlene that only his known piety saved him from the suspicion that he was her father.

In addition to the sense of personal loss that Morlene is to sustain, she must contend with her grief over the approaching death of a man whose sweetness of soul and fatherly care had won from

her almost a daughter's love. With hands clasped
like unto one supplicating, she strains her beautiful eyes, as if, in her solicitude, to watch the soul
along the whole distance of its flight into the great
unknown.

Standing here and there in the room are dis-
tinguished white neighbors, intimate friends, ready
to testify that the noblest Roman of them all is
passing away.

In an adjoining room, still other white neighbors
are recounting in undertones the many noble deeds
performed by Maurice Dalton. Huddled together
under the trees in the yard to the back of the
house are the Negroes of this and other planta-
tions, who, with woeful looks, peer anxiously in
the direction of the "big house," eager for news as
to how the battle was going. The vitality of Maurice Dalton was surprisingly great, and he grappled
with this "last of foes" far longer than had been
deemed possible. Probably it was his unfulfilled
promise to Morlene that caused his spirit to linger
here so long after it had received the final summons.

Morning wore away into the afternoon. The
air grew humid and signs of coming rain multiplied; yet the Negroes stood their ground, determined to be as near as possible to their beloved
landlord in the supreme moment.

Dark clouds which, ascending from the horizon, had been curtaining the skies, now passed beneath the sun, intercepted his kindly rays and journeyed onward until not a patch of blue was anywhere to be seen. Excitedly the lightning displayed his fierce glance in the disturbed heavens, first here and then there, and the occasional mutterings of the thunders were heard.

The Negroes at last mustered sufficient courage to make the attempt to have Maurice Dalton to die, if die he must, in what they regarded as the ideal manner. Any Negro that could die "happy," die in the midst of a frenzy of joyous emotions, was deemed by the mass of Negroes as assured of an entrance into heaven. In order to produce this condition of ecstasy, they would gather about the bedside of the dying and sing such songs as were calculated to deeply stir the emotions of the passing one. They now concluded to use their singing upon Maurice Dalton. Leaving the shelter of the trees they all drew near to the house and stood under a window of the room in which lay the dying man.

In plaintive tones, low, timorous and wavering at first, then louder and bolder, in sweetest melody, they sang:

> "Swing low, sweet chariot,
> Cum fur ter carry me home;
> Swing low, sweet chariot,
> Cum fur to carry me home."

Ofttimes as a boy Maurice Dalton had stood on
the outer edge of Negro open air camp meetings
and had heard, with deep emotion, this chant;
and as the music now comes floating into his room
his paroxysms cease, a smile plays upon his face
which, though wasted, is handsome still.

Suddenly he sat bolt upright in his bed.
"Hush!" said he, feebly waving his hand, as he
turned his ear in an attitude of listening. "Did
they say the chariot had come?" he enquired of
the weeping Aunt Catherine. Casting a faint look
of recognition on those who stood near him, he
fell back upon the bosom of Aunt Catherine—a
corpse.

The wild cry of anguish that escaped the lips of
Aunt Catherine told its own story to the Negroes
in the yard. The singing ceased and they turned
to go. Tears were falling from their eyes, and
Nature, as if in sympathy, began to weep also.
In after days the minds of the Negroes oft reverted
to the darkness and gloominess and utter dreari-
ness of the day when Maurice Dalton died.

CHAPTER II.

"A NEW KING. . .WHICH KNEW NOT JOSEPH."

"Morlene, you and Catherine will come into the library as soon as your breakfast duties are over."

Such was a command addressed to Morlene by Lemuel Dalton while he was sitting at the breakfast table in the Dalton house, a few days subsequent to the happenings recorded in the preceding chapter.

Morlene passed out of the dining room into the kitchen to tell Aunt Catherine what Lemuel Dalton had said. But Aunt Catherine had heard for herself and was so much agitated by what she thought were sinister purposes revealed by his tone of voice, that she began to tremble violently. A plate which she was washing fell to the floor and broke, whereupon she whispered to Morlene in tremulous tones:

"Dar, now! I shuah knows dar is trubble brewin' 'round 'bout heah. Las' night I drempt 'bout snakes an' didn't git to kill 'um. All dis mornin' my right eye hez been jumpin' fit to kill, an' now I dun broke dis plate. W'en hez Aunt Catherine broke er plate afo' dis? Shuah's yer bawn, chile, dar is trubble brewin' in dis 'neck ub

(15)

de woods.'" In a still lower whisper she said: "I wondah whut debbilmint our young marster's got in his he'd ter sen' fur us?"

Morlene, who was also apprehensive, shook her head slowly, signifying that the master was an enigma to her as well.

After the lapse of a few minutes, Aunt Cather ine and Morlene repaired to the library, where they found Lemuel Dalton tilted back in his desk chair, his hands clasped behind his head. Turning the gaze of his gray eyes full upon Aunt Catherine and Morlene, who were sitting together, he began:

"Both of you are aware of the fact that I am now the proprietor of this place. I have one more task which I wish to perform as plain Lemuel Dalton. I will be rid of that task to-day, I think. To-morrow I intend assuming charge here. I shall have no Negroes whatever about me, and the two of you will please prepare to leave when I take charge to-morrow."

Aunt Catherine groaned audibly at the announcement and her dilated eyes showed that she viewed the suggestion with a species of horror. Morlene was self-contained, being careful not to exhibit any emotion, if she felt any. Lemuel Dalton, desirous of preventing an outburst of grief from Aunt Catherine, hastened to say:

"You will go from the place well provided for. I find, according to my uncle's memorandum, that there are six hundred and forty-eight dollars to your credit, money which was due you, but not called for by you. I notice that you have been accustomed to give largely to objects of charity, else this sum to your credit would be the larger. You will find the amount in this package." So saying, he lightly tossed the package into her lap.

"Morlene, I find a note in my uncle's memorandum which states that you are entitled to be cared for by the Dalton estate so long as you live. I know not what is the ground of your claim, nor do I care to know. I shall see to it that you do not suffer. Understand, however, that you will always apply to my lawyers for aid and not to me. With this one thousand dollars which I now hand to you, our personal dealings come to a close."

He tossed the package of money, which was in currency, toward Morlene, but she took pains to see that it fell upon the floor and not upon her lap. This was done so adroitly that Lemuel Dalton did not know but that the failure of the package to reach its destination was due to his poor marksmanship.

Aunt Catherine asked in broken tones: "Marse Lemuel, will yer 'mit me ter say er word?"

A frown of impatience appeared upon Lemuel Dalton's brow, but he nodded assent.

Aunt Catherine stood up and began:

"Marse Lemuel, I wuz bawned on dis place. I wuz brung up hear ez a chile, and all de fun an' frolics I ebber hed wuz right heah. Marse an' missus 'lowed me an' my ole man ter marry heah. It was in front ub dis very house whar us, my ole man an' me, jumpt ober de brum stick es a marrige cerimony. Since I hez been an 'oman ebry baby bawn in dis hous'' hez cum in ter dese arms fust. Yer own daddy Erasmus wuz one ob um, an' a lackly littul fellah he wuz, too. Dese hans you see heah hez shrouded de Dalton dead since I ken ricermimber. Durin' war times, w'en udder darkies wuz brakin' dey necks ter go ter de Yankees, I staid right by missus an' I'se been in dis house ebber since.

"Nachally, Marse Lemuel, I lubs dis spot. I jes' doan' know nuthin' else. I hed hoped to die heah an' be bur'i'd at de feet ub missus, for she promis' me wid her dyin' bref ter let me wait fur de trump ub Gabrul by her side. Now, Marse Lemuel, doan' dribe me erway. I'll wuck an' not charge nary cent. I wants to stay whar I ken plant flowers on de grave ub Maury an' de rest. Gib me er cot an' let me sleep in de ole barn lof' whar I played ez er gal; but doan' dribe me erway."

Here Aunt Catherine burst forth into sobbing.

Lemuel Dalton's frown deepened. He arose and walked to the window, his back to Aunt Catherine, who now dropped upon her knees to pray for God to reinforce her plea.

Lemuel turned, and discovering Aunt Catherine in an attitude of prayer, said: "That is all unnecessary, Catherine. My mind is made up. I do not mean to be unkind, but I simply shall not have Negroes about me."

Aunt Catherine finished her prayer and arose. Taking the money which Lemuel Dalton had given her, she said in gentle tones: "Whut I did fur our folkses wuz fur lub. You shan't spile my lub by payin' me fur whut I hez dun." So saying, she walked over to Lemuel Dalton in an humble attitude and dropped the package of money at his feet. She then turned and went slowly and disconsolately out of the room, her head drooping as she shuffled along.

Morlene, who had manifested great self-control during the whole of the affecting scene, now arose and boldly faced Lemuel Dalton.

"Sir," said she, her eyes filled with tears, "it takes no prophet to foretell that terrible sorrows await you! He who ignores human emotions, will find many in this world more than a match for him at his own game! As for the money which you gave me, I shall not touch one penny of it. Really, I do not care to have my life linked by means of the smallest thread to a man who shall come forth from the 'mills of the gods' ground as you will be. You have not my anger, sir, but my most profound pity." So saying, she, too, left the room.

Lemuel Dalton was seized with a nameless, indefinable terror, that caused his blood to grow chill; and in that instant the consciousness came to him with the certainty of a revelation that Morlene had spoken the truth. But this feeling only remained for a few seconds. It was but a forerunner, years ahead of its time. He cast it off, seeking to assure himself that belief in a premonition was but an idle superstition. When he had fully recovered his composure he said :

"Now, I like that plucky spirit manifested by the girl. Give me, every time, the haughty sufferer, too proud to crouch beneath the lash even when its sting is keenest. I want none of your whining suppliants. A plague on these Negroes who meet injury with woe-begone expressions. That sort of thing tends to make the Anglo-Saxon chicken-hearted in dealing with them. The more a Negro whines and supplicates the worse I hate him. But I tell you I like the spirit of that girl." Such was Lemuel Dalton's soliloquy.

"But other tasks await me," he said. Taking a pistol from his hip pocket, he thoroughly examined it to see that it was in prime condition in every respect. Satisfied on this score, he put it back into the pocket from which he had taken it. Going out to the stable, he mounted his horse and rode away, taking the road that had been made to pass through and connect the several parts of the vast Dalton estate. On every side of him were tokens of what the forces of nature were doing for him. The earth holding in her bosom the roots of acres of Indian corn, was yielding up her substance that the grain might ripen unto harvest. The stalks were bravely bearing the swelling ears. The beautiful drooping blades drank in the contributions that the sun and the air had to bestow.

Thus all nature was at one working for the welfare of the future master of the Dalton place. But he had no eye for nature's loving panorama. A master passion had his soul within its grasp.

CHAPTER III.

A FALLEN MAN SHOOTS.

About one dozen years prior to the time of the beginning of our story, Lemuel Dalton, then a lad, was fishing on the banks of a body of water known as "Murray's Pond." The scene surrounding it was one of extreme loveliness, and Lemuel, though a child, was yet poet enough to be silent while nature was speaking to him so eloquently and yet so soothingly. There was the shining sun above bathing the scene with its summer warmth. There were the trees standing around, lazily luxuriant, surfeited. Wild flowers of varied hues were present in great profusion, as much as to say, "See, this is not so bad a world after all, else we could not be here." The trees that stood near to the pond cast their shadows upon its clear waters and saw with satisfaction themselves mirrored therein. A few cows had come to the pond and stood in one section thereof, the embodiment of contentment, leisurely tinkling their bells. Lemuel was absorbed in the contemplation of this scene.

A Negro boy, about Lemuel's age, but much larger, was fishing on the other side of the pond.

The scenery had no charms for this boy, who, tiring of the monotony of unsuccessful angling, decided to leave his side of the pond and engage in a conversation with Lemuel.

When he drew near, Lemuel paid no attention to him, not so much as casting a glance in his direction.

Nothing daunted by this seeming indifference, the Negro boy attempted to start up a conversation. "Good place to fish, ain't it?" he said.

Not a muscle in Lemuel's face moved.

Drawing a little closer, the Negro boy touched Lemuel on the shoulder, and with a smile said, "Good place to fish, ain't it?"

Lemuel moved away, neither speaking to nor looking at the boy.

The Negro boy now got angry, and, throwing his fishing pole across his shoulder, started away, saying with a sort of lilt that resembled singing:

> "I like sugar,
> I like hash,
> I'd rather be a nigger
> Than poor white trash."

This was the taunting reply used by Negro children to avenge insults, real or imaginary, coming from white children. It was tantamount to a declaration of war, and was everywhere regarded as a *casus belli*, and Lemuel Dalton accepted it as such.

He sprang to his feet and was soon engaged in a fisticuff with the Negro boy, who, however, proved to be his superior and signally defeated him.

Lemuel Dalton, the man, is on his way to see this Negro, now also a man. It is his purpose to settle this old score before assuming charge of his estate on the morrow. We shall now acquaint you more fully with his prospective antagonist.

There lived on the Dalton estate a Negro of middle age and medium height, who bore the name of Stephen Dalton. In his youth he was a slave of the Dalton's and remained on the place after the coming of freedom. Sober, industrious, thrifty, thoroughly honest, peaceably inclined, he enjoyed to a remarkable degree the esteem of the white and colored people of all classes.

Maurice Dalton was only nominally the head of the Dalton estate, the practical operations of his farming affairs being entrusted to the care of this Negro, Stephen Dalton.

Stephen Dalton's household consisted of himself, a son and a daughter, his wife being dead. It was this son, who years ago, had had the fight with Lemuel Dalton. Harry Dalton, for such was the son's name, was now a very handsome, vigorous looking young man. He was conscious of his acceptable personal appearance and was somewhat vain. This vanity was not lessened, of course, by his knowledge of the fact that he was the best farm hand in all that section of country. He was, however, very companionable, and his uniformly cheerful disposition made him a sort of favorite with all, in spite of his touch of vanity He had attended the public school located in his vicinity, and while not very proficient, had succeeded in mastering about all that the teacher could impart.

On this particular day. Harry has abandoned his field duties, and, watched by his very devoted sister, Beulah, is engaged in practice in order that he may be in prime condition for the sports incident to the coming of an excursion from the neighboring city to a nearby grove. Harry was the champion runner, jumper, boxer and baseball player, and was quite eager to maintain his proud distinction.

Beulah, who stood in the doorway of the three-room farm house in which they lived, said to Harry, "Look behind you! Yonder comes old Lemuel Dalton!"

Harry glanced over his shoulder, but did not desist from his practice.

Lemuel Dalton rode up to where Harry was, dismounted, hitched his horse, and came directly in front of Harry.

Since their fight at Murray's Pond the two had not spoken to each other, and both now understood that a fight was to ensue. In a biting tone Lemuel Dalton began :

"I suppose you know that I am owner of this place. I have come to lay down my law to you. You are the leading sport on the place. Regardless of the condition of crops you quit to go to picnics, shows, dances, camp meetings, funerals, and on every excursion that comes along. Your example is demoralizing to the whole farm. I assume charge of this place to-morrow, and I want you to understand that you cannot go to the picnic scheduled for that day."

Harry was fairly enraged that a white man should speak to him as though he were a slave. Before he could suppress his anger enough to trust himself to speak, Beulah cried out from the door:

"Don't that beat you? Some poor white trash that gets places by the death of their uncles don't know that Grant whipped Lee and Jeff Davis was hung to a sour apple tree."

Quivering with rage, Lemuel Dalton said to Harry: "You apologize for what that girl has said."

"She has spoken my sentiments," said Harry.

The two now began to prepare for battle. Lemuel Dalton advanced toward Harry and began the conflict with a stinging blow on Harry's left cheek. The battle was then on in earnest. Harry had the advantage in point of native strength. Lemuel's reach was longer than that of Harry, and he was by far the more skillful. He had for years been taking boxing lessons secretly, that he might be prepared for this very occasion. Lemuel Dalton had the further advantage of coolness. Harry, allowing his emotions of anger to influence him too largely, struck out wildly and thus dissipated much of his strength. Lemuel's wariness in evading Harry's onslaughts and skill in delivering blows added to Harry's irritation.

As the battle progressed it began to dawn on Harry that somehow he had met with more than his match. The thought of being defeated by Lemuel and in the presence of Beulah was too galling, and Harry determined to prevent such an outcome at all hazards. In a fit of exasperation, and in return for a well aimed blow from Lemuel, Harry delivered a powerful kick in his abdomen. Lemuel staggered backward and fell to the ground, Harry rushing toward him.

"Is that your game?" shouted Lemuel. Half raising himself by means of his left elbow, with his right hand he drew his pistol in time to shoot Harry just as the latter was about to throw himself upon him. Harry now fell to the ground seriously wounded.

Beulah came rushing to Harry's side screaming loudly.

"That comes of insulting poor white trash," said Lemuel Dalton, as he mounted his horse. As he turned to go he cast a look of triumph and contempt at the wounded Negro and his screaming sister. Beulah's cries brought help from the field near by, and strong hands bore Harry into the house.

CHAPTER IV.

THE CLANS GATHER.

News of the fight between Lemuel Dalton and Harry Dalton soon spread throughout the surrounding regions. The diffusion of news was so rapid because in the country each person regarded himself as a courier in duty bound to convey word to his immediate neighbors. The white farmers abandoned their tasks, armed themselves and hurried to the Dalton house.

At nightfall the Negro farm hands from far and near hastened to Stephen Dalton's home, secreting in their clothes such weapons as pistols, hatchets, razors, bowie knives, clubs, etc.

Thus, what was originally a personal encounter between two individuals contained the germs of a race war.

When a sufficient number of the whites had gathered at the Dalton house to justify it, an informal meeting was held in the large front room. 'Squire Mullen, a short, fat man, with a face of full length but somewhat narrower than it might have been, assumed the leadership of the meeting. His upper lip was shaved clean, while his chin supported a beard about three inches long. He spoke in a quick, jerky fashion, addressing Lemuel Dalton in the name of the assemblage as follows :

" We have heard of the difficulty between you and one of the darkeys on your place. We have come to learn from you the particulars about it, to find out just what action must be taken by us. We are not seeking to interfere with your affairs, but darkeys must be made to feel always that whatever any one of them does to one white man is considered as done to all white men; we shall be pleased, therefore, to receive any information that you may see fit to give."

In response to this address Lemuel Dalton gave to the assemblage a full and truthful account of the happening. When he was through, 'Squire Mullen sprang to his feet saying, " Permit me, sir, to voice the sentiments of my fellows. We did not come here to sit in judgment on your action. We came here under the inspiration of the Anglo-Saxon motto, which is summed up in these words, 'My country, may she be always right. But, right or wrong, my country.' We came here, sir, to take up your cause; but your account shows that you have struck us a blow in the face—square in the face."

" You will, of course, explain your remarks," interposed Lemuel Dalton, in a tone which signified his non-acceptance of 'Squire Mullen's view of matters,

"Certainly, certainly, sir. In the midst of circumstances such as exist in the South, the greatest force that makes for peace is the cultivation in the white man of a sense of superiority and in the darkey a sense of inferiority. Engender in the darkey a sense of his inferiority and it will paralyze his aggressiveness and do more to keep him down than a standing army. What we practice in the South is racial hypnotism. We erect signs everywhere, notifying the darkey of his inferiority. To be effective this work must be co-operated in by practically the whole body of white men. That's why we object to any white man's attempt to disabuse the Negro's mind of this sense of inferiority. You, sir, have acted in a manner to cause us to lose the aid of this sense of inferiority in dealing with our darkeys. You have made our task of controlling them the harder. You have thus done us harm and the darkeys harm."

"You have not yet shown how my actions transgress your mode of procedure," said Lemuel Dalton.

"Why, sir, you fought the darkey on terms of equality. You fought him man to man. You should have sat on your horse and scolded him. If he had spoken insultingly, you should have used your horsewhip on him. If he had proven dangerous, it was your duty to have shot him without further ado. A fisticuff between a white man and

a darkey savors too much of equality, a feeling
that must be kept out of the Negro at all hazards."

"Permit me to add a word," requested a feeble-
voiced young man, rising in a most timid manner,
rubbing his hands together nervously.

'Squire Mullen gave him a reassuring look and
he proceeded,

"I simply wish to reinforce what 'Squire Mullen
has said by a historical incident.   On a certain occasion when the Scythians were returning from a
war in which they had been engaged, they received
news that the servants whom they had left behind
had mutinied and taken possession of the city and
the households of their former masters. The
Scythians were preparing to attack the slaves with
a full accoutrement of arms when one of their
number protested. He told his fellows that the
best way to conquer the slaves was to discard arms
and go with whips simply. He held that arms
would suggest equality, while whips would be a
reminder to the slaves as to what they were. The
experiment succeeded and the Scythians effected a
re-enslavement without any bloodshed. So, I agree
with 'Squire Mullen that it is a great help to superiors to keep alive in inferiors a well developed
sense of their inferiority. It certainly helps to
keep them in subjection. The Scythian whips,
which had as an aid the feeling of inferiority, were
more successful than arms would have been, carrying along with them the idea of equality.

"A profound thinker of our day sets forth this idea in these words:

"'There are the respective mental traits produced by daily exercise of power and by daily submission to power. The ideas, and sentiments, and modes of behavior, perpetually repeated, generate on the one side an inherited fitness for command, and on the other side an inherited fitness for obedience; with the result that, in course of time, there arises on both sides the belief that the established relations of classes are the natural ones.'"

The young man dropped into his seat and looked around rather bashfully and wistfully, hoping that he would be regarded as having made an acceptable contribution to the dominant thought of the occasion.

All eyes were now directed to Lemuel Dalton, awaiting his reply.

"Gentlemen," said he, "if you will but go a little deeper into the subject you will see that my action was in accordance with and not contrary to the philosophy which you enunciate."

There was a slight bustle of astonishment at this claim, but Lemuel proceeded without regard thereto.

"When I was a lad, that Negro insulted and then beat me. No doubt he carried with him for years the thought that he was physically my superior. I was determined to wrest from him this conception. Had I proceeded against him on terms which he regarded as unfair, he would not have inwardly restored to me the palm which he wrested from me years ago. But, proceeding against him on terms of equality as I did, he is forced to acknowledge in his innermost consciousness that I am physically his superior. I, for one, think that we white men make a mistake in not seeking by physical culture to maintain even our physical superiority. I am in favor of the doctrine of Anglo-Saxon superiority in all realms, even the physical."

'Squire Mullen, with a smile upon his face, came forward and grasped Lemuel Dalton by the hand.

"We understand you better now, sir. We are proud of you, sir. Lads, hear what he says. In developing brain don't forget brawn. The darkey now has brawn. His strong physique and reproductive powers, show that he is in the world to stay to the end of time. If, in the years to come, he adds mental to physical endowment, we may be in the lurch unless we take care of the physical side of our development. Give me your hand again, sir," said 'Squire Mullen, once more shaking hands with Lemuel Dalton.

This matter having been disposed of, consideration was now given to Harry and Beulah. It was the concensus of opinion that the education which Harry and Beulah had received was mainly responsible for what the whites termed "arrogant assumption of equality."

The advisability and inadvisability of educating the Negro was gone into and the conclusion reached that the only safe education for the Negro was the education that taught him better how to work. It was decided that Harry had been punished equitably for his offense against Lemuel Dalton as an *individual*. They held that something must be done however, to avenge the insult to the white *race*, perpetrated when one of their number was assailed.

As a result of their deliberations, lasting well up into the night, it was decided to drive Harry and Beulah out of the settlement, both as a punishment for their offense and as a warning to other Negroes against "impudence towards their superiors."

In the meanwhile the Negroes had been coming and going at Stephen Dalton's. They came in part from curiosity, in part to see if they were in danger, and in part out of sympathy. They all listened critically to Beulah's recital of the trouble.

The practically unanimous verdict was that Beulah and Harry could and should have avoided the conflict. Arriving at this conclusion they all left, not being disposed to help in a case where all of the blame was not on the white man. In the dead of the night the whites rode up to the house and tacked thereon a notice, warning Harry and Beulah Dalton to remove from the settlement forever before the dawn of day on the first of January of the incoming year. When the Negroes heard of this decree they were incensed.

"Ernuf is ernuf," said one. "An' a nigger ain't er dog. 'Twuz ernuf ter shoot de nigger. We didun't do nuffin' 'bout dat, kase de niggers wuz some'ut ter blame. But dey ez carrin' de thing too fur. Ernuf is ernuf!"

This sentiment was universal among the Negroes, and they decided, one and all, to retaliate by leaving the settlement along with Harry and Beulah.

About thirty miles distant was the city of R——, the great commercial center of all the surrounding sections. This city now became the Mecca of these Negroes. But other troubles were to ensue ere they accomplished their design to enter R——.

CHAPTER V.

BREEDS TROUBLE FOR AFTER YEARS.

When Lemuel Dalton rode into his yard fresh from his encounter with Harry Dalton, Aunt Catherine and Morlene were in a wagon ready to be driven to the city, where it was there purpose to dwell.

Lemuel Dalton noticed the look of inquiry which his battered appearance evoked from Morlene's expressive eyes, and, as if to prevent her from thinking that he had been worsted and that her prophecy was already coming true, said in a haughty tone: "I do not know how much interest a knowledge of the fact may be to you, yet, I inform you that I have just shot down that impudent Negro, Harry Dalton.

Morlene was of a deeply sympathetic mould, and, upon receiving this information, tears came into her eyes. Alighting from the wagon, she said: "Go! Go! Aunt Catherine, from this accursed place. I will come to the city soon. It may be that Harry is not killed. If I can save his life I can ward off that much of the terrible debt that this man is piling up against himself." Gathering her skirts about her, weeping as she ran, she arrived at Stephen Dalton's house and assumed charge of the nursing of Harry.

Harry's wound was an exceedingly dangerous one, but the doctor's skill, supplemented by Morlene's zealous care, eventually brought him to a stage of convalescence. But Morlene's tenderness of heart had brought her into a situation where unforeseen complications arose to sorely disturb her peace of mind.

So, soon as Harry became conscious of Morlene's presence in his home as his nurse, he began to look upon his being shot as an especially kind act on the part of providence. From early childhood he had been an ardent admirer of Morlene, but her stay at the Dalton house under the guardianship of Maurice Dalton, had caused him to feel that there was an impassable gulf between them. He had never been able to summon sufficient courage to go up to the "big house" with the intention of paying his respects to Morlene. He now entertained not one spark of ill will toward Lemuel Dalton for shooting him, since it was the means of drawing Morlene to his side. The scrupulous care and great tenderness exercised by her in the nursing of Harry, were construed by him to be indications of a strong attachment, and his hopes of a favorable outcome of his suit grew greater from day to day, until he at last regarded his acceptance as an assured fact.

One day, after he was able to sit up, he beckoned for Morlene to come to his side, intending to make a declaration of love. Morlene came and looked into Harry's face tenderly, awaiting his request, which she presumed would be upon some matter in line with her duties as a nurse. When Harry looked up into her face, so tenderly beautiful, his heart failed him. " Too beautiful for a fellow like me," he thought. "I have changed my mind, Miss Dalton," said Harry, abandoning his purpose for the time being.

Morlene looked at Harry out of those wondrous eyes of hers, playfully feigning reproach, shaking her forefinger at him the while, in no wise dreaming of the emotions at work in Harry's bosom.

The day at last came when Harry found himself possessing sufficient courage to make a declaration of love. It was indeed a rude awakening for Morlene when she realized in what manner she had been the object of Harry's thoughts, a contingency upon which she had in no wise calculated. When her emotion of surprise had sufficiently abated to permit it, she told Harry in a very pleasant manner that he was sick and should wait until he was well before giving attention to so grave a question as marriage.

Harry had discerned how his proposal had surprised Morlene, and he now knew that she had not given him one thought as a possible husband. He saw clearly that Morlene's many acts of kindness to him were based purely on sympathy, not love. This so discouraged Harry that it was not many days before he began to grow worse. His decline was so persistent, refusing to yield to any treatment, that the doctor was sorely puzzled as to the cause of the relapse and the treatment necessary to effect a change.

Harry's illness now reached such a stage that all began to despair of his life. Beulah kept constant watch at his bedside, noting his every expression. She noticed how Harry's eyes followed wherever Morlene moved about in the room; how that he was restless when she was out of sight and contented when she was near. And in all this devotion exhibited by Harry she intuitively felt the presence of hopelessness. She framed the theory in her mind that the mysterious cause of Harry's decline was none other than an unrequited love for Morlene.

The doctor came, felt Harry's pulse, shook his head, and left the room. Beulah also went out and revealed to him her thoughts.

"By Jove!" said he, "Why did I not think of that myself? The girl is as beautiful as a sylph. She can save him, I am sure. That boy's relapse can be explained on no other hypothesis. See what you can do with the girl. It is the only hope left." So saying, the doctor went his way.

Beulah now re-entered the house and asked Morlene to take a walk with her. Arm in arm the two girls went down the little pathway leading from the house. Coming opposite to a grove of trees they turned toward it, entered, and sat down upon a fallen log.

"Morlene, are you in love with any one?" asked Beulah.

"No, my dear. Why do you ask?" replied Morlene.

"I have a request to make of you, which I can the more freely do since you say that you are not in love."

Morlene's face took on a puzzled expression.

"What possible relation does my not being in love bear to any request that you might make?" inquired Morlene.

"The doctor has told me that the only hope of saving Harry's life lies in your consenting to marry him. He is dying of love for you," said Beulah.

Morlene stood up affrighted.

Beulah continued: "Harry looks at you so sadlike. A word from you, Morlene, will save him."

Morlene sat down and raised a hand to her forehead. "Beulah," said she, "I fear that there is something in what you say. I now recall that his decline in health began about the time when I refused to consider a proposal of marriage which he made. But Beulah, I do not *love* Harry. I think well of him, but I do not love him."

"You could learn to love him," said Beulah.

"No, I am quite sure, Beulah, that I could never love a man on Harry's order. Something within tells me that somewhere in the world there is an ideal man that awaits my coming. He shall awaken all the slumbering fires of my soul and my life shall entwine itself about his. Beulah, I believe all this with my whole heart."

Morlene spoke in tones quavering with emotion, her beautiful face showing signs of tragic earnestness and her eyes assuming a far-off expression as if the soul was seeking to divine the future.

"Morlene, you and I are poor country girls and can talk plainly to each other. You have been reading books up at the Dalton house which set forth the deeds of mighty men. Out of all that you have gleaned from books you have constructed your ideal man whom you feel awaits you in the world. Morlene, we country girls have only a limited education and know but little of the requirements of the higher walks of life. The man whom your imagination has selected will be so much your superior in point of culture that he will not notice you."

This was a well directed shaft and Morlene's body twitched as if it had been entered by some deadly missile; for it had been the one dread of her life that the man whom she could love would consider her mind too poorly trained to become his companion. Morlene buried her face in her hands.

Beulah followed up the advantage which she saw that she had gained, saying :

"Morlene, your own judgment must teach you that your ideal is impossible of attainment. Put over against this impracticable ideal my honest, industrious, wounded brother, who is being destroyed by his love for you. Do not, Morlene, allow poor Harry to die because of a vague hope."

A pet squirrel which had been tamed by Harry, and which was very fond of him, was jumping from limb to limb in a neighboring tree. Spying Morlene and Beulah, it began to descend, making looks of inquiry at various stages of its journey. Upon reaching the ground, it began to hop in the direction of the two girls, halting now and then to turn its little head first one way and then another, always keeping one or the other of his brown eyes looking in their direction. When only a few feet from them, it reared upon its hind feet and looked intently at them. They were evidently too sad in appearance, for it immediately scampered away to resume its sport.

"Even the squirrel has come to plead for Harry, Morlene," said Beulah.

Morlene's answer was a deep sigh.

"Beulah," said Morlene, taking her hands from her face, "you hardly know what you ask. This love which God has planted in a woman's bosom is the source of the highest joy that she knows during her stay on earth. You are asking me to surrender the most precious gift of my Creator, my one chance of supreme happiness."

Beulah now burst into crying, calling into play woman's most formidable weapons—her tears.

"All right, Morlene. Poor Harry will be dead to morrow, and I shall soon die of grief. You know how my dear father loves us. Our deaths will break his heart. When we are dead, Morlene, remember that the surrender of an idle hope on your part would have saved us all."

Beulah, weeping bitterly, now arose to go. Morlene's sympathetic nature could not longer resist the strain.

"Beulah, Beulah, it is hard to do as you ask. How hard, the future alone can tell. I consent to sacrifice myself. I don't understand this world, anyway! Why am I placed in such a trying situation? I will marry Harry!"

It was now Morlene's time to cry. She wept bitterly, her gentle spirit chiding the cruel fate that had woven such a web about her feet. Parentless, homeless, friendless, now doomed to a loveless marriage, she considered her lot an inexpressibly hard one.

The two girls wept together, Beulah now weeping over the necessity of imposing such a marriage on Morlene. Having as Harry's sister persuaded Morlene into agreeing to the marriage, she now as a woman wept in sympathy with Morlene over a prospective wedlock without love. When the two had regained self-control, they returned to the house. Morlene went to Harry's bedside and knelt there. She took his enfeebled arm and laid it across her shoulder, smiling at him sweetly the while.

"Harry," said she, "I have come to tell you that I am going to be your wife, a true wife—one that will do all that is in her power for your comfort and welfare."

So saying she leaned forward and sealed her doom with a kiss.

Beulah, eager to insure Harry's recovery, and fearing that Morlene, after a period of reflection, might deny the binding force of a vow extorted from her in the dread presence of death, hastened matters. The next day Harry and Morlene were duly pronounced man and wife.

When a woman's hand is chained and her heart is free!

CHAPTER VI.

AN ACT OF WHICH NOBODY IS PROUD.

The decision reached by the assemblage of Negroes in the first burst of excitement over the posting of the notice demanding that Harry and Beulah leave the settlement, was adhered to, and on Christmas Eve several wagon loads of young Negro men and women started on their journey to the city. The crops had been marketed and each one had come into possession of the profits on his year's labor. In no case was the amount very large, but it caused all to be in good cheer.

The occupants of the wagons were as numerous as the wagons could well hold, and they rode standing up, holding to each other to keep from falling whenever the uneven character of the road caused the wagons to jolt. A jug of whiskey had been placed in each wagon and from it bottles were filled and passed around, men, women and children alike taking each a "dram." Loud laughing, playful bantering, sallies of coarse wit, ribald singing, characterized this journey to the city. The more sober and religious element of the Negroes, who were disgusted with this sort of conduct, stayed behind to avoid contact with those inclined toward

(46)

rowdyism. They wished also to improve the occasion by holding one more service of worship in their country church house.

On Christmas morning the church was filled with those who had come to worship God there, perhaps for the last time. The minister was expected to preach a sermon appropriate to the occasion. Recognizing this expectation, he sought to fulfill it, and chose for his text, Hebrews xi:16:

"But now they desire a better country, that is, a heavenly: wherefore God is not ashamed to be called their God: for he hath prepared for them a city."

The preacher began his discourse in that deeply pathetic tone accompanied with prolonged mournful cadences, once so largely in vogue among a certain class of Negro preachers. This tone, so full of the note of sorrow, found responsive chords in the bosoms of his hearers and a bond of fellowship for the occasion was at once established between him and them. His every utterance was saluted with an answering groan or sympathetic manifestation of some kind, evoked as much by the tone of voice as by the sentiment expressed. The responses of the people heightened the emotions of the preacher. Thus the preacher and the people acting and reacting upon each other, produced a highly emotional state of affairs.

The burden of the preacher's discourse was an account of the wanderings of Abraham and the subsequent sorrowful career of his descendants in the land of Egypt. With a constantly swelling tide of emotions the hearers followed the dolorous account, which was made the more touching by instituting comparisons, the purport of which was to show that the Negroes were having similar experiences. In drawing to a close, he emphasized the thought that the God that prepared a goodly land for the Jews would take care of the Negroes. He urged them to leave the question of their earthly welfare in the hands of God and center their thoughts on Heaven. He entered into a dramatic description of the Christian's getting ready to wade across the Jordan of death.

Then came a vivid word painting of the scenes beyond—the green fields of Eden; the pearly gates standing ajar; the gold paved streets; the jasper walls; the tree of life; the long white robes; the silver slippers; the starry crown; the palms of victory; the harps of gold. The Christian was to go into the city, he set forth, and sit upon a throne singing God's praise, looking out of the window of heaven while the sun was covered with sackcloth and ashes and the moon was dripping away in blood.

His very last remarks were made sitting down, in representation of the final rest of the Christian in the midst of the stirring scenes depicted.

The tumultuous scene which accompanied and followed this highly dramatic peroration beggars description. Women screamed and shouted and fainted, while men wept like babes and clambered from seat to seat wild with emotion. Such was the character of the religious preparation that the Negroes had for the grave responsibilities of life in the city. While these things were transpiring at the church, a frightful tragedy was being enacted elsewhere. A short outline of the circumstances leading up thereto is now necessary.

When the white farmers became aware of the fact that there was to be a wholesale exodus of Negroes from the settlement, they were much enraged. They recognized the fact that the Negro made a very good laborer, in spite of his foibles, and they were loth to let him go. Their course toward him was not, as they understood it, dictated by prejudice nor tainted with injustice. They were thoroughly imbued with the doctrine that they were inherently superior to the Negro and instituted repressive measures to keep alive recognition of this claim. This was the Alpha and Omega of their purposes, and they were angered, that their course, to them righteous, should be accepted in any other spirit, and should operate to disturb the social fabric. They argued with the Negroes, endeavoring to show them that they were not opposed to Negroes *per se*, but to "sassy" Negroes that tried to put on airs and represent themselves to be as good as white people. All efforts to stem the tide of emigration failed, however.

Lemuel Dalton alone was undisturbed by the outcome. Years before, as the prospective land-lord of the Dalton place, he had made a careful study as to how he could operate the plantation without the aid of Negroes. He had come to the conclusion that the presence of the Negro on the farm lands of the South, was the chief cause of its backwardness. He looked upon the Negro as being of too conservative a mold, averse, like all primitive people, to innovations. He had given earnest study to improved meth-ods of farming and had determined upon many changes that would dispense with much labor. He had in mind to substitute barbed wire for rail fences and thus be rid of Negro rail-split-ters. Improved plows, planting, threshing and harvesting machines—in fact, the whole category of labor-saving devices for farming were to be brought into use. By thus elevating farm life from a condition of extreme drudgery he felt hope-ful of securing white farm hands to take the place of Negroes. So the contemplated exodus did not in the least affect Lemuel Dalton's peace of mind.

Not so with other young white men of the set-tlement, yet living on their fathers' places. In view of a prospective scarcity of "hands" they had been notified that they would have to abandon their lives of ease and help to man the farms. The thought of performing the drudgery incident to

farm life was very distasteful to them, and they became very bitter in their feelings toward the Negroes.

On this Christmas morning, a number of these
young white men went to the one whisky shop in
the vicinity to drink off their troubles. As they became intoxicated, their fury rose until it was evident that trouble of some sort was certain to ensue.
One of the drunken lot said, " Boys, what say you ?
Down with the cause of all our troubles ! What
shall we do with Beulah Dalton ?"

"Kill her ! Kill her ! Kill her !" rang out
from the throats of the half-drunken crowd.

With much yelling and hooting, they started
toward Stephen Dalton's home. Beulah had always been disliked by the young white men, as
she persistently refused to speak to any of them
that did not call her " Miss Beulah." This long
nourished feeling of animosity was no doubt a factor, though unconsciously so, in the present movement against her.

Beulah had remained at home, while the others
went to the church. She was completing her
preparations for the journey to the city, to take
place on the morrow. She heard the wild shouts
drawing nearer and nearer, and looked out of her
window to discover the meaning thereof. The
crowd caught sight of her, and with a yell of sav-
age delight, came toward the house at full speed,

Beulah had the presence of mind to barricade the doors. The windows were furnished with thick oak doors that closed from the inside and effected a protection for the apertures supplementary to that of the window panes. These doors Beulah closed.

When the crowd arrived at the house they found Beulah securely ensconced. As their doings were not premeditated, they had come from their homes without implements with which to batter down the doors. Finding their purpose of capturing Beulah thwarted, they were under the necessity of providing another mode of procedure.

"Burn her up!" said one.

"You are a coward. The gal ain't no rat. Give her a chance, fool," replied another.

"Who calls me a fool?" shouted the first speaker. "I will kill the scoundrel," he added.

A wrangle here broke out and a free for all fight was threatened, some favoring one of the disputants and some the other. While they were engaged in this drunken squabble, one of their number had gotten into the kitchen and had saturated the floor with kerosene oil. He then set fire to the building.

Beulah heard the roaring flames and decided to make a bold dash for life. She was a country girl, vigorous of frame and fleet of foot and hoped to

outrun the crowd in their drunken condition.
Quietly unpinning the barred door, she leaped out
and began to run. She chose the side of the house
opposite to the one where she heard the noise, and
supposed that at least a short interval would in-
tervene before the crowd discovered that she had
escaped.

But the young man who had set the house on fire
had gone to that side of the house in anticipation
of an attempt to escape. When he saw Beulah run
forth from the building, he uttered a yell and with
great effort of will steadied himself sufficiently to
hurl at the fleeing girl a stick of stove wood which
he had gotten in the kitchen. The stick struck
her on the back of her head. Beulah fell forward
and in a few minutes breathed her last. When the
Negroes returned from church, they found the ashes
of the house and, a short distance away, Beulah
lying on her face in a puddle of blood. The
perpetrators of the crime had fled.

CHAPTER VII.

A MAN AGAINST A REGIMENT.

Stephen Dalton, whose conservatism was proverbial; who had been from time immemorial the assuager of race animosities; who had so successfully mediated between the whites and the Negroes at every previous crisis, was at last thoroughly aroused to action. The ills of which the Negroes had complained, and concerning which he had always counseled moderation, were now brought home to his own door. As a result of the race feeling his son had been wounded, his house burned, the friendly relations of a lifetime destroyed, and his daughter, the pride of his heart, murdered while at home unprotected. With his gun on his shoulder he tramped from house to house for miles around exhorting the Negroes to repair to a designated spot where they would march in unison to attack the whites.

The Negroes felt that the time for action had assuredly come if "cool headed" Stephen, as he was called, was aroused to the point of action. Their long pent-up feelings of resentment now became rampant and they gathered in force at the point selected by Stephen. They came armed with such weapons as they could buy, borrow or steal.

The white people of the settlement became thoroughly alarmed; for, though the Negro was regarded as a normally peaceful being, they felt that there was a latent sanguinary nature and a sort of reckless dare-devil bravery that burst forth upon occasion and was dangerous. They telephoned to all nearby stores, requesting that firearms and munitions of war be denied to all would-be Negro purchasers. Word was sent to neighboring settlements to guard the crossroads and prevent other Negroes from different sections coming to the assistance of those already in arms.

The telegraph and telephone stations were put under strict censorship, and all newspaper reporters were warned to send out no accounts of the trouble that would create the least vestige of a doubt as to the entire justice of all the proceedings of the whites.

Messages were sent to the governor that a race riot was imminent, and an urgent plea was made for several companies of State troops. These were forthwith dispatched.

The whites who had armed themselves, now joined the ranks of the State troops to assist in quelling the uprising of the Negroes. There was no desire among the whites for bloodshed, and, being fully prepared for war, now cast about for a means of bringing about peace.

The usual mediator, Stephen Dalton, being the leader of the Negroes, they had to search for another. They decided to impress into their service for that task the Negro public school teacher.

The Negro school teacher has perhaps been the greatest conservator of peace in the South, laboring *for* the Negroes by the *appointment* of the whites, being thus placed in a position where it was to his interest to keep on good terms with both races. Thus the whites on this occasion sent the school teacher to confer with the Negroes.

Arriving at the Negro assemblage the teacher approached Stephen Dalton.

"Good evening, sir," said he to Stephen.

"Good evenin'," was Stephen's gruff response.

By this time a number of Stephen's lieutenants had clustered around the two, eagerly looking from the teacher to Stephen and from Stephen to the teacher, bent on catching whatever might pass between them. They made no attempt to conceal their feeling of curiosity, which was as manifest as in the case of children.

"May I be allowed to address this gathering?" asked the teacher of Stephen.

"Whar is you frum?" queried Stephen, grumly.

"I have just come from the white people's rendezvous," he replied.

"Thought so. Bettah go back dar, I 'specks," said Stephen, turning his back and walking away.

The teacher now turned to the others who had crowded about him. "Men," said he, "I have something to say that concerns you all. Uncle Stephen is interested in this whole affair in too personal a manner for you men to commit your interests blindly to him. In times like these you need a man who is in such a frame of mind that he can weigh everything. Now, you all know that Uncle Stephen has had enough to unbalance anybody, and, I tell you, men, unbalanced minds are not safe guides in such times as these."

The men gathered about the teacher now looked in the direction of Stephen. He, seeing that the teacher was engaging the attention of the crowd, decided to return and order him away.

"I is cummander in chief, heah, sur, and you mus' leave dis groun' at once, sur," said Stephen to the teacher.

The teacher now lifted his voice and said in tones that many could hear.

"In former times when other people's oxen were gored, Uncle Stephen was not driven away when he came to see you. Uncle Stephen is a good man, but I don't think he is that much better than the rest of you. If *your* matters could be talked of, it seems to be that *his* might be talked of, too."

This blow was well aimed. There seems to be a feeling in the Negro race to keep all upon a level and to resent anything that savors of superiority of one Negro over another. No man who attempts to lead them can have any measure of success unless

he is thoroughly democratic in his behavior, tastes
and manner of approach. The teacher knew of
this feeling, and his remark was an adroit bid for
its support.

The Negroes now felt a little sullen toward
Stephen Dalton, their commander, because he desired to prevent free speech on this occasion when
he had availed himself of it so often in times of
threatened trouble.

"Uncle Stephen is in a mighty heap of trouble,
an' ain't 'zactly at hisself. Go er head, teacher,
we'll hear you," said one.

A murmur of approval went through the crowd,
which had now swelled to large proportions.

Seeing that he had gained audience the teacher
began. In his speech he set forth that the killing
of Beulah was not indicative of the feelings of the
best white people toward the Negroes, nor of the
real feelings of the worse elements of whites. He
said that liquor was at the root of the murder,
and that in a measure the colored people were
responsible, because it was their vote that kept
liquor from being voted out of the county at a local option election held a short while previous.
To this the Negroes nodded assent, for they knew
it to be true. The teacher asked why, as sensible
people, they were going to have all the folks of
the community, good and bad, white and colored,
killed for an act that liquor was mainly responsible
for, they being responsible for the liquor.

Then the teacher recited the facts as to the superior training, numbers, equipment, transportation facilities, means of inter-communication of the whites. He dwelt upon the fact that the Negroes were practically cut off from all other Negroes, and the battle would really be between that little handful of Negroes aud the whole body of white people of the South. The teacher spoke earnestly, and impressed the throng that he was doing them a service in calling their attention to their hopeless plight.

When the teacher was through his hearers were won over to his way of thinking.

Stephen Dalton had foreseen what would be the outcome, knowing from experience how susceptible the Negroes were to argument at such times. Before the teacher had concluded he dropped his gun and ammunition and walked away quite rapidly. Arriving at the place where the white soldiers were stationed, he pulled off his coat, rolled up his sleeves, clenched his fists, stepped forward and spoke as follows, his eyes gleaming with rage:

"Gentlemens, the man whut you done sent up yonder will turn them people, an' I reckin it's best. Dare aint no use'n er whole lots er folks dyin' fur me one. Now I wants to make a fair propursition ter you."

Stephen's voice grew loud and strident.

"My house is burned, my boy is shot, my gal is killed, an' me all broke up at dis age. Gentlemens, justis' comes in som'ers. Uv course nairy one man uv you could stan er show befo' me, fair fist an' skull fight. Pick out any two men an' sen um to me an' I'll lick um. Gentlemens, on dat plan I'll take the whole regurment uv you. Now, gentlemens, I ax yer in de name uv justis, consider my propursition. Ef you think that ain't fair, I'll take any three uv yer fair fist and skull."

Stephen now awaited an answer.

The whites, who at heart sympathized with Stephen in his grief, regarded him as unbalanced by trouble. No one replied, and there was no thought of harming him.

"Ah! Gentlemens, you kill er pore gal when her daddy wuz erway, but you won't fight him, I see. Gentlemens, dare uster be bettah blood dan dat. I was in de war wid my marster, an' he showd good blood to de Yankees. Is it all gone, dat three uv you won't fight ur 'nigger,' ez you call him?"

By this time the teacher had arrived, accompanied by two friends of Stephen. They came to report that the Negroes had disbanded and would give no more trouble. Stephen's two friends now approached him and stationing themselves on either side, begged him to leave.

The old man's head drooped upon his bosom. He had at last collapsed, having been so long under a severe mental strain. His two friends supported him between them and bore him from the spot,

Stephen repeating over and over in a broken voice: "Boys, dey don't fight fair. Dey don't fight fair, boys. Beulah! Beulah! your daddy can't do nuthin'. He would if he could. Boys, dey won't fight fair."

The Negroes *en masse* now gathered up their few belongings and removed to the city of R—— with all of its aggregation of vice, of temptation, of hardships, of alluring promises, of elusive hopes.

As they enter this typical American city, we fain would follow them, but cannot just now. May the fates deal kindly with them.

CHAPTER VIII.

THE HINT NOT TAKEN.

The eyes of the civilized world were now directed to the settlement wherein Beulah was murdered, in order to witness there the workings of the
sentiment of justice.

The poet's pen, the artist's brush, the sculptor's
chisel, have long since despaired of adequately
setting forth the natural charms of the Southland,
the home of birds and flowers, grand with mount-
ains, beautiful with valleys, restful in the girdling
arms of her majestic streams, presided over by skies
that are the bluest of the blue.

Knowing the proud place given the Southland
by the fiat of Nature, the world of mankind riveted
its gaze upon her eagerly and pressed to know the
fate of those who murdered Beulah. The great
heart of the South throbbed with a sense of shame
over the perpetration of the crime and now sought
to shake itself loose from the benumbing influences
of an ever-pervading race feeling that was so powerful as to render inoperative so many higher sentiments. The pulpit and the press spoke in terrible
tones to the hearts and consciences of the whites
in denunciation of the crime and in demand that
the guilty parties be brought to trial,

In addition to their natural horror of the crime, the best white people of the South had another incentive for desiring that they should act worthily in the matter. The white people had arrogated to themselves the right of exclusive control of public affairs. This act had been quietly submitted to by the Negroes, and the people of the North at that time appeared to be disposed to accept in great measure the Southern white man's view of his own problem. With all that they demanded practically conceded, they felt the more under obligations to make human life within their borders safe and sacred.

The Governor of the State offered large rewards for the apprehension and conviction of the perpetrators of the crime. In spite, however, of all the indignation of the South, no arrests were made. The members of the mob were in some way related to practically every influential family in the county in which the crime had been committed. In many cases the prosecutors would have found themselves proceeding against their closest kin.

The coroner's jury, duly impanelled and sworn, viewed the remains of Beulah and brought in the stereotyped verdict that "the deceased came to her death at the hands of a party or parties to the jury unknown." This verdict brought the incident to a close, so far as society, acting through legally constituted agencies, was concerned. But the incident was not in reality closed; for when a given agency fails to adequately meet the demands of humanity, the people find a way of making their power felt. Public sentiment began to mete out, in its own peculiar way, the justice which the courts had felt unable to administer.

The young men who had committed the crime, found themselves ostracized on every hand. Those who were engaged to be married, received notes cancelling their engagements.

When the people so elect they can make a citizen's garb burn into the soul of a man with an intensity equal to that of prison stripes. If the perpetrators of the crime were not convicts, the difference would not have been discovered by a comparison of their feelings with those of real convicts.

It came to the ears of 'Squire Mullen that his son Alfred had been the one to apply the torch and to strike the blow that brought on Beulah's death. The 'Squire was the soul of honor, as he understood it, and while he believed it to be the design of God that the white man should keep the Negro in a subordinate place, he yet deemed it an unspeakable horror to needlessly afflict a helpless people.

'Squire Mullen went to the room of his son on the night of the day on which he had heard of the part that the young man had played in the matter. The hour was late; his son was asleep in bed. The father said to himself as he looked at his sleeping offspring :

"I do not yet know that my boy is *that* guilty. Let me stroke those Saxon curls and kiss his cheek once more before I find out whether or not he is guilty." His caressings awoke Alfred, and the tenderness died out of the 'Squire's face, a look of stern justice mounted the throne.

He said : "Alfred, news reaches me that you applied the torch to Uncle Stephen's house while his daughter was in there, and that you struck the blow that killed her. I have come to know of you, my son, as to whether you did or did not do these things."

Alfred sat up in bed, a look of deep remorse upon his young and handsome face.

"Father," he said, "I would give the world to be able to truthfully say that the statements are false ; but I cannot. The statements are true, too true !"

'Squire Mullen's eyes closed, his features became pinched, a harrowing groan escaped his lips. In his heart, honor and justice were throttling the love of his son. The moment was as excruciating as the soul of man ever knew. The struggle was great, for the opposing forces were great ; but the conflict was of but a moment's duration.

'Squire Mullen turned and dragged himself out of the room. His step was no longer elastic. That instant had brought on the old age which his energetic will had persisted in delaying. In a few minutes he returned, bringing with him the family pistol. He placed it on the lamp-stand that stood at the head of Alfred's bed. Without saying a word he left the room. He went to bed, but, alas, could not sleep. He lay throughout the night ex·pecting a sound that failed to come. When the fowls in the barnyard began to signal the approach of day, he arose and went to Alfred's room again. He said, "Alfred ! Alfred ! Alfred !" Alfred awoke.

"Can you sleep on such a night?" said the 'Squire, in tones of agony. "Is the family honor that low also ? Can we thus bear open disgrace ? Alfred ! Alfred ! There is a pistol at the head of your bed." So saying, the 'Squire returned to his room to again listen for the sound that would have been the most welcome of any that could be made.

Alfred now understood that his father desired him to commit suicide. He grasped the pistol and held it in his hand. He longed at that moment for the courage to die, but it was missing. He had been brought up from infancy by a "black mammy," and she had succeeded in imbuing his soul with her living fear of hell and her conceptions of a personal devil. As he sought to lift the pistol to his head, vivid pictures of lurid flames and grinning demons arose and paralyzed the hand that he desired to pull the trigger. Day broke and he was yet alive.

The 'Squire now came and took the pistol from the table where Alfred had replaced it, saying not a word to his son. That day he summoned all of his relations that were near by to gather at his home. In response to his request they came, their wives and daughters accompanying them.

In the middle of the afternoon the men repaired to the front yard, leaving the women in the house. It was somewhat cold and a bonfire was started to keep them warm. A circle of chairs was formed around the fire and the men sat down, two chairs having been put within the circle to be occupied by 'Squire Mullen and Alfred. These two now took their seats side by side. A huge leather back book was in the 'Squire's hands. His face wore a stern aspect, but one could tell that grief born of love was gnawing at his vitals. Since the previous night his hair had whitened and his brave eye had lost its glitter. He arose to address the meeting. Opening the book which he had in hand, he said : "Kinsmen, I hold in my hand the record book of the Mullens. I shall on this occasion read to you a terse statement of the most notable achievements of the Mullens from the time of William of Normandy until the present."

They all listened attentively while he read, Alfred's eyes being cast upon the ground.

Having traced the family history to his own generation, the 'Squire read of the deeds of prowess of himself and the others assembled who had rendered excellent service to the cause of the Southern Confederacy. When through with this he called the name of Alfred Mullen.

The 'Squire paused, then said: "Kinsmen, it would appear that I must now record the deed of one who claims to be my offspring and a partaker of the blood of our illustrious family. If so be, then the record must read that Alfred Mullen, on a *Christmas* morn, murdered a Negro *girl* in the absence of all *male* protection. The murder was *unprovoked*, and committed by Alfred Mullen while he had the protection of a gang of his fellows.

"Kinsmen, I have summoned you here to know if this deed must go on record. If you decide that it shall not go on record, you know what that means."

Turning to Alfred, he said: "It means that you must abandon the name of Mullen upon pain of being killed; that you must never lay claim to kinship with us; that you must go forth with the mark of Cain upon your brow."

The 'Squire now took his seat. There was a short pause. Then one by one the relatives arose and, with becoming gravity, made speeches repudiating Alfred, insisting that his sin against the traditional honor of the house of Mullen was unpardonable.

Before taking a final vote, Alfred was asked as

to whether he had anything to say. He made no reply; his head was still bowed. A vote was then taken and Alfred stood expelled from the Mullen family forever.

The assembly now adjourned, and all the men, save Alfred, returned to the house, where sat the women in silence and in sorrow. Alfred, the outcast, had gone. When the men entered the room Mrs. Mullen read in their countenances the fate of her boy, and she uttered a short, sharp scream of anguish that she could not repress.

"Mourn not for Cain," said 'Squire Mullen, whose twitching face belied the sternness of his voice. His heart, too, was sadly, cruelly torn by what had befallen his boy, but as best he could he maintained an outward calm.

That night a mob was formed at 'Squire Mullen's house. In silence the men proceeded to the barroom where their sons had imbibed the inspiration for their nefarious crime. They dragged out all of the kegs and barrels containing liquor, and emptied the contents on the ground. They then set the building on fire, and it was soon an ash-heap. A committee waited upon the barkeeper, reimbursed him for his losses and warned him to never more sell liquor in that settlement.

CHAPTER IX.

DORLAN WARTHELL.

A few years subsequent to the events recorded in the last chapter, in the city of R——, where our country friends had gone to live, on a sultry summer evening, near sunset, Morlene went forth into the front yard of her home for the purpose of watering her flowers. She had on an evening gown, while her head was hidden in a bonnet. With her back to the street, she stood leveling the water from the hose at the various flower groups. While she was thus engaged, a man above the average in height, possessing a form that conveyed the impression of nobility and strength, was in the act of passing by. When he came directly behind Morlene, having a keen relish for nature's supreme efforts at the artistic, he was so struck with the outlines of her form that he involuntarily stopped.

"Now that is what I call beauty," he exclaimed, without knowing that he spoke.

Morlene vaguely felt that some one had stopped, the fact of the cessation of the footsteps dawning upon her consciousness. She turned full around and her eyes fell on the handsome face of the man gazing at her. His skin was smooth, his features regular, his eye intelligent and his head so formed as to indicate great brain power. As to color he was black, but even those prejudiced to color forgot that prejudice when they gazed upon this ebony-like Apollo. Wherever he appeared he was sure to attract attention as a rare specimen of physical manhood. His was evidently an open, frank nature, and his soul was in his face.

As Morlene looked upon him she felt her strength give way. The hose fell from her hands. Her very soul sent up a wail: "Alas, O God, there he is! Why did you let him come?" She turned and fled to her house.

Dorlan Warthell, for such was the name of the man, was much discomfited that he had so terrified the lady, and resolved at some convenient time to apologize for the shock that his behavior had caused. He entered the yard, stopped the waste of water from the hose and proceeded on his journey, carrying in his mind the image of the most beautiful woman on whom he had ever laid eyes.

Morlene on entering her room, locked the door, burst into tears, buried her face in her hands, sobbed violently. Judge her not too harshly, dear reader. Allow her this brief moment of weeping over the re-opened grave of her long buried ideal; for, one glance at Dorlan Warthell, say what you will against love at sight, had somehow sufficed to tell her penetrating spirit that he was the

one man, who, had she been free, could have ex-
acted that full strength of love, which, struggle as
painfully as she might, would not yield allegiance
to Harry whom she had married under a species
of duress. Morlene dropped her hands from her
face, forced a smile to appear, stamped a pretty
foot upon the floor and said between gritted teeth:
"Avaunt, ye idle dreams of youth; I am a woman
now, a man's lawfully wedded wife! Come not
here to haunt me with visions of what might have
been!"

When Harry came home from his work that
evening Morlene met him with a greeting of more
than usual warmth, as much as to say, "Poor Harry, your place in my heart is the safer, now that
my dreams of other days have been met in con-
crete form and gloriously vanquished." She now
consoled herself with the thought that she would
one day love Harry as she had always desired to
love a husband. Happy in this thought, she retired
to rest, and, much to her chagrin and annoyance,
dreamed of the handsome stranger whom she had
seen.

CHAPTER X.

CUPID SHOULD BE MORE CAREFUL.

"This is a matter worthy of investigation," mused Dorlan Warthell, some few moments after his chance meeting with Morlene. His head was inclined forward slightly, an unwonted sparkle was in his eye, and half a smile played upon his serious face. His mind was seeking to grasp the outlines of that beautiful face which he had just passed.

"Never," said he, "has Dorlan Warthell, the serious, allowed physical beauty to so charm him. But is it mere physical beauty that has so suddenly thrown itself across the pathway of my mind so that it will not move on? Has nothing met me more than that lovely form, the head of a queen, angel face, eyes that thrill? I may be mistaken, but methinks that nature has given that choice dressing to a choice spirit. At any rate I hope to meet her again."

Dorlan Warthell arrived at his boarding place within a few minutes and, when seated at the supper table, spoke as follows to Mrs Morgan, his landlady : "I notice that our street has some new denizens since the time of my sojourn here a few years ago."

"Yes," replied Mrs. Morgan, "There are Mr. Crutchfield, Mr. Yearby and Mr. Dalton. These gentlemen have all come to this street since you were with us last."

"Who lives in that beautiful cottage painted white, with that wonderful assortment of prettily arranged flowers in the front yard?"

"Mr. and Mrs. Dalton live there," replied Mrs. Morgan, looking intently at Dorlan, seeking to fathom the secret purpose which she felt inspired his question ; for she knew that Dorlan paid but little attention to the matter of houses and neighbors.

"Have Mr. and Mrs. Dalton any children—a daughter?" asked Dorlan, giving strict attention to the food on his plate.

"No ; they are childless," said Mrs. Morgan, her interest growing.

"I saw a young woman up there as I passed this evening ; I suppose she is a visiting them."

"I see the point—a young woman," said Mrs. Morgan inwardly.

Aloud she said, "Perhaps so. If you could describe her I might be able to tell who she is."

Dorlan looked up quickly as much as to say, "Who in the world can describe that beautiful woman." He kept that reflection to himself. He began to describe the lady, when Mrs. Morgan interrupted him to say.

"Oh, that was Mrs. Dalton—Mrs. Harry Dalton—undoubtedly the most beautiful Negro girl in the country."

Dorlan finished his meal in silence. He inwardly belabored himself for having allowed his mind to be so taken up with the image of a married woman. Repairing to his room, he was soon deeply engrossed in a book, as thoroughly oblivious of Morlene, he thought, as if he had never seen or heard of such a person.

On the following day at ten o'clock Morlene called at the residence of Mrs. Morgan, it being her usual time for giving music lessons to that lady's young daughter. The girl had gone away on an errand for her mother and had not yet returned. Morlene entered the music room and decided to amuse herself by playing until the child should come. Dorlan was in a room directly over the one in which Morlene was to play. Neither of them knew of the presence of the other in the house.

Morlene first began to play a light air upon the piano. But as she struck the keys and brought forth harmonies, other and deeper emotions in her bosom craved for expression. Soon she was making the piano tell her heart's full story, to be borne away, as she thought, upon the wings of the passing breeze. The sounds floated up to Dorlan's open window and into his room. At first he slightly knitted his brow, fearing that he was to be bored by some mechanical performer; but the frown relaxed and gave place to a look of supreme contentment as the harmonies deepened. He closed the book that he was reading, folded his arms and gazed out of his window into the distance. He was simply enraptured and had a keen desire to know who it was that could make lifeless matter pay such eloquent tribute to the longings of the human soul.

At length Morlene began to play and sing:

> " John Brown's body lies moulding in the clay;
> John Brown's body lies moulding in the clay;
> John Brown's body lies moulding in the clay,
> As we go marching on.
> Glory! Glory! Hallelujah!
> Glory! Glory! Hallelujah!
> Glory! Glory! Hallelujah!
> As we go marching on!"

Morlene's voice was a rich soprano and her tones were so round, full and melodious that they made one feel that they did not belong to earth. Her voice seemed to shake loose from each word tremblingly in that part of the song setting forth the sad fate of John Brown. But as she reached the words, "Hallelujah," the notes swelled into a grand pean of triumph, her voice trilling so wondrously, even upon such a high elevation. Then came the refrain in low, reverential tones, beauty muffling itself in the presence of higher sentiments.

Dorlan Warthell sprang to his feet, clasped his hands over his ears, saying half aloud : "Spare me! Oh, spare me! I cannot, I cannot hear those strains and perform the tasks before me. And yet I must! I must! I must!"

Charles Sumner, who, upon the floor of the United States Senate, in tones that resounded throughout the world, urged our Republic to clear her skirts of the blood of the slave ; Horace Greeley, who, daily in the columns of his great newspaper, refused sleep to the American conscience until slavery was extirpated ; Henry Ward Beecher, whose eloquence across the seas quieted the growlings of the British Lion all but ready to aid the South ; these three men, ere they fell asleep, saw fit to abandon the political party under whose banner they had hitherto fought.

And now Dorlan Warthell felt called upon to do likewise. On the eve of the severing of his tender relations, some angel voice has come to serenade his soul and conjure up the hallowed past. Ah! 'tis painful when the path of duty must be paved with one's heart strings. It is also sometimes strewn with one's blood.

CHAPTER XI.

A STORMY INTERVIEW.

On a night shortly subsequent to the day on which the playing and singing of Morlene had so greatly affected Dorlan, he had a visitor.

"How goes it, Dorl, old boy" said his visitor, slapping Dorlan on the shoulder familiarly.

"I am doing well, I hope, Congressman Bloodworth. Accept a seat in my humble quarters," Dorlan replied. Congressman Bloodworth dropped into a chair, crossed his short legs and began stroking his red mustache.

Congressman Bloodworth was a white man, with an abnormally large head and a frame somewhat corpulent. His complexion was sallow and his skin very coarse. His eyes were large but exceedingly tame in appearance. He lifted his hat from his head revealing an abundance of hair of a brilliantly red hue.

Dorlan took a seat at some little distance from Congressman Bloodworth anticipating that the interview was not to end pleasantly.

"Well, Dorlan, I have come for my answer," said Congressman Bloodworth in his gross voice.

"Mr. Bloodworth. when we were last together I

gave you to understand very fully what to expect of me. Nothing has transpired since to cause me to change and I am sure that I shall adhere to the course which I have chosen, unto the end," said Dorlan, in a pleasant but most positive manner.

"Dorlan, have you a memory?" queried Congressman Bloodworth.

Dorlan nodded assent.

"Then bear me witness, sir." So saying he took from his pocket a typewritten document, which he proceeded to read.

He began, "From the year 1619 until January 1, 1863, the Negro race wrs subjected to slavery in the United States. The superior numbers, greater intelligence and determined spirit of the enslavers prevented the enslaved from cherishing any hope of setting themselves free. The great task of redemption which the Negroes saw no way of accomplishing for themselves, the Republican party accomplished for them at a cost of much treasure and of hundreds of thousands of precious lives. This party enacted such laws as made a recurrence of slavery absolutely impossible. It clothed the freedman with the rights of a citizen. It extended to him the strong arm of the Federal Government in the protection of those rights. The claim that these facts establish over the allegiance of every Negro, I leave to the judgment of any sane mind,

So much for the relationship which by implication should exist between *you* and the political party named.

"I now advert to my own peculiar claims upon you. Your early years you spent in school and received great mental development. You found employment as a stable boy in the home of an eminent statesman. During your leisure hours you perused his library and became thoroughly imbued with the spirit of the statesman. Owing to your residence in the South, there was no outlet for your powers, as the South was not permitting men with black faces to aid in running the government. By accident we met, you and I. I discovered that you had great talent. I was lacking in native ability. I decided that, as you had the necessary brains and I the white face, we might form a combination. You planned, I executed; you acquired information, I exhibited it. By your secret aid I went to Congress. Through you I arose from the ranks to a commanding place in the public eye. For the past few years my speeches in and out of Congress have been regarded as so full of merit that they have been used as highly acceptable campaign documents. These speeches were composed by you. In return for your furnishing me brain I have paid you every cent of money which I have received as compensation for public service. Making use of my white face you have been able to allow full play to your intellect, which delights in grappling with great questions.

"Dorlan Warthell, I come to you to-night with this carefully prepared statement, that I may secure your final answer. Will you or will you not continue working through me and for the Republican party?"

Congressman Bloodworth folded the paper from which he had read and looked steadily at Dorlan.

Dorlan replied, "Congressman Bloodworth, I am thoroughly convinced that the Republican party is in error in the chief tenet of its present day creed. My devotion to truth is far greater than my devotion to party. And, Mr. Bloodworth, it was truth that set my people free. The Republican party became the willing instrument of truth to effect that result. Now that the result has been achieved, I must not confound the power with its instrument. I worship at the shrine of truth, not at that of its temporary agents. My spirit is free to choose its own allegiance, for no human instrumentality has freed my spirit; its freedom came from God."

"Sir," spoke out Congressman Bloodworth, "You deny my and the Republican party's authority over you, in spite of what we have done for you?"

"I assert that no event in the history of the world has yet happened that makes it my duty to follow error," said Dorlan vehemently.

"You shall die the death of a dog," shouted Congressman Bloodworth in rage.

The two men had now risen and were glaring fiercely at each other. Congressman Bloodworth looked as though it would please him to tear Dorlan to shreds; but Dorlan's powerful, well constructed frame was too potent an argument against such an attempt.

Congressman Bloodworth turned away and left the room. Murder was in his heart and stamped its impress on every lineament of his face.

CHAPTER XII.

MORLENE AND DORLAN.

The day following the night of the stormy interview was Morlene's day to give lessons at Dorlan's boarding place. The teaching over, Morlene proceeded to amuse herself by playing on the piano. She was in a buoyant mood and was disposing of first one and then another wild, dashing air.

Desirous of a diversion, Dorlan came down from his room and glided stealthily into the parlor to listen unobserved to Morlene. Great was his astonishment on discovering that the beautiful lady whom he had passed was none other than the accomplished pianist and divine singer. For a few moments he lived a divided existence, his eye surveying the beautiful form of Morlene, while his ear was appropriating the rich harmonies which her splendid touch was evoking from the keyboard.

With a merry laugh at her own frolicsomeness, Morlene struck the piano keys a farewell blow and arose to go. Wheeling around she saw Dorlan. The light died out of her face. A feeling of terror crept over her as the thought occurred that fate, relentless fate, seemed determined to throw that fascinating stranger in her pathway.

"Do not be angry with me for my intrusion," said Dorlan. "My soul is the seat of a long continued storm these days, and your music was so refreshing," he continued.

Dorlan's air of deference and his pleasing, well modulated voice caused Morlene to at once recover her composure.

The note of sadness in Dorlan's voice caught Morlene's ear and her sympathetic nature at once craved to know his troubles that she might, if possible, dissipate them. She saw that Dorlan was depending upon her to begin a conversation as an assurance that he had given no offense. Morlene sat down in the seat nearest her.

"You speak of a storm," she said. "When you speak thus you arouse my interest, for to my mind a storm is the most sublime occurrence in nature. To see the winds aroused; to hear their mad rushing; to behold them as with the multiplied strength of giants they grasp and overturn the strongest works of man's hands—to see this, inspires one with awe and reverence for the great force that pervades this universe, and impels us, whether we so will or not, to conform to its ripening purposes.

"If there is a storm in your bosom, matters exterior to yourself have produced it. As an admirer of storms I beg you to lay bare to me such portions of the journeyings of the winds as a stranger may be permitted to view."

"Do you believe in strangers?" asked Dorlan, "I hold that no human beings are, at bottom, strangers to each other. With Emerson I hold that 'there is one mind common to all individual men. Every man is an inlet to the same and to all the same. Who hath access to this universal mind is a party to all that is or can be done, for this is the only and sovereign agent.'

"Those souls are quickest to recognize this fact which are best equipped to reveal themselves and to comprehend the revelations of other souls. We know some souls at a glance as thoroughly as one soul ever knows another."

To these observations Morlene made no reply. Too well did she know that the human being before her, was somehow, no stranger to her.

"Starting out with the assumption that you shall find nothing strange in me when you fully understand me, I am ready to show you the pathway of the storm," continued Dorlan.

"Thank you," said Morlene, smiling, and partially revealing a set of teeth as beautiful as fair lady ever desired.

"A presidential election is fast approaching. I have heretofore labored with the Republican party. In this campaign I part company with them," said Dorlan.

"My dear sir," said Morlene, rising, the picture of excitement, "Are you a Democrat?"

Dorlan smiled at the intensity of the feeling displayed in the tone of voice used for the question. "Oh, no," said he, reassuringly. "In the South, Democracy's chief tenets are white man's supremacy and exclusiveness in governmental affairs. Not having a white skin, self-preservation would prevent me from entering the folds of that party."

Morlene heaved a sigh of relief. She said, "I am glad to know that the seeming hopelessness of our plight in the South has not caused you to seek to influence us to surrender to this dictum of Southern Democracy. Proceed, if you please."

"I am thoroughly displeased with the policy of the Republican party toward the inhabitants of the Philippine Islands, and in spite of the endearing relations of the past, I am moved to part company with the party on this issue," remarked Dorlan.

"Oh, I am an enthusiastic expansionist, Mr. —— ."

"Warthell is my name," supplied Dorlan.

"Mr. Warthell," said Morlene, the glow of eloquence on her face, "I have a dream. I dream that wars and revolutions shall one day cease. The classification of mankind into groups called nations, affords a feeling of estrangement which destroys or modifies the thought of universal brotherhood, and gives rise to the needless bickerings

which result in wars. I delight in any movement
that sweeps away these pseudo-national boundaries.
The more separate nations that are congealed under
one head, the less is the area where conflicts are
probable. When the tendency to consolidate finally merges all governments into one, wars shall
cease. Our territorial expansion is but the march
of destiny toward the ultimate goal of all things.
I am delighted to see our nation thus move forward,
because we have such an elastic form of government, so responsive to the needs and sentiments of
the people that bloody revolutions become unnecessary wherever our flag floats. Just think how
much our expansion makes for universal peace by
erasing the thought of separateness existing between peoples, and giving to the federated powers
such an ideal form of government.

"When our flag floats over the whole of the
Western Hemisphere there will be nobody over
here to fight us; we shall not fight among ourselves
and we shall dare the European and Asiatic powers to go to war."

"You are indeed an expansionist," remarked
Dorlan.

"Yes, yes," said Morlene, wrought up in the subject that was stirring the American people.

"Some are expansionists for the sake of finding
outlets for the ever-increasing excess of our produc-
tion. They hold that we are producing far more

than what we can consume, and must have outside buyers to avoid a terrible congestion at home. Others are expansionists on the ground that outlying possessions are a strategetical necessity in the time of war. Our statesmen are expansionists, some of them, because our nation's becoming a world power gives a broader scope for their intellects. Some are expansionists because they desire to see weaker people have the benefits of a higher civilization. While I admit the possible weight of these various contentions, my interest in expansion is broadly humanitarian. England was at one time a seething mass of warring tribes. The expansion of a central power over the entire islands brought order out of chaos. Let the process extend to the entire earth as fast as honorable opportunity presents itself, and may the stars and stripes lead in the new evangel of universal peace" Thus spoke Morlene.

"Beautiful, beautiful dream. But it is my fear that enthusiasm over expansion may cause us to lose sight of fundamental tenets of our political faith. This leads me to state the point of difference between myself and the Republican party," said Dorlan.

The subject was one, as may be seen, of absorbing interest to Morlene, and she leaned forward slightly, eager to catch each word that Dorlan might utter. He began: "The Republican party has not informed the world as to what will be the ultimate status of the Filipino. In the final adjustment of things, whatever *that* may be, will the Filipino be able to say that he stands upon the same plane, politically and otherwise, with all other free and equal human beings. I labored earnestly to have the Republican party to declare that no violence would be done to our national conception that every man is inherently the political equal of every other man. The party has promised that full physical, civil and religious liberty shall be guaranteed. On the question of political liberty there is silence. Because of this silence I leave it."

"In what manner, Mr. Warthell, do you hope to affect the result in the pending campaign?" enquired Morlene.

"The Negroes, you know, are vitally affected by the issues in this campaign. With England imposing its will upon India, with the Southern whites imposing their will on the Negroes, only one great branch of the white race exists which is not imposing its will upon a feebler race. I allude to the white people of the North.

"Should our nation, by the force of arms and without the promise of ultimate political liberty, impose its will upon the Filipinos, the weaker peoples the world over will lose their only remaining advocate in the white race, namely the people of the North.

"I hope to be able to show the Negroes that they, of all citizens in this country, cannot afford to permit either silence as to, or the abandonment of, the doctrine of the inherent equality of all men. The Negroes of the pivotal states, when, united, can easily decide the election in whatever direction they choose. It is my purpose to attempt to weld together the Negroes in the hope of defeating any man that will not unequivocally and openly declare in favor of the ultimate political equality of the Filipinos."

"Are you not leaning on a broken reed, Mr. Warthell?" asked Morlene in earnest tones. "Have the Negroes acquired sufficient self-confidence to feel justified in pitting their judgment against that of the Republican party? Can the recent beneficiary be so soon transformed into a dictator? More important still, can you uproot those tender memories which flourish in the sentimental bosom of the Negro, associating, indissolubly his freedom with the Republican party?" she asked.

Dorlan sighed deeply. He recalled how madly he had to fight against the tender memories aroused by Morlene's singing when we saw him so deeply stirred. He remembered how that on that occasion her playing and singing had carried his mind back to those great days when the freedom of the Negroes was in the balances. He knew what an effort it required on his part to persuade his heart to allow him to strike a blow at that hitherto hallowed name—Republican.

Dorlan not replying, Morlene resumed, "Mr. Warthell, in attempting to disillusion the Negroes with regard to the Republican party you shall march against one of the strongest attachments in all of human history. I have known deaths to result from assailing attachments far less deep-seated than that. May a special providence preserve you."

Morlene now arose to go, her beautiful face giving signs of the fear for Dorlan's safety that had stolen into her heart.

Subsequent happenings showed how well grounded were her fears.

CHAPTER XIII.

A WHOLE CITY STIRRED.

The editor of one of the leading morning papers of R—— sat at his desk one afternoon, knitting his brows as he read a document spread out before him. Having finished reading it once, he began the second reading, wearing on his face the same intent expression. Having concluded the second reading, he laid the article down, rested his head on the back of his chair and closed his eyes as if in deep meditation. After a few moments' reflection he decided upon the third reading of the document. When he had finished this last perusal, he went to the telephone and summoned Dorlan Warthell to an immediate conference with him. Dorlan soon arrived and was ushered into the editors's private office.

"Be seated," said the editor, in a most cordial manner. "Mr. Warthell," said he, "I have read your document the third time and I now desire to ask you two questions. The character of your answers to them will determine whether I shall propound to you a third." Looking earnestly into Dorlan's face, he enquired, "Was it your desire and expectation that this article should be published?"

"Most assuredly," said Dorlan, manifesting surprise that the editor should deem it necessary to ask such a question.

"Again," said the editor, "are you well acquainted with the moods of your people?"

"It is my impression that few men have studied them more earnestly than I have," said Dorlan.

"I see that I must ask my third question. Thinking that your article would be published, knowing your people, have you exercised foresight enough to have your life insured? If you have not, fail not to do so to-night; for a straw in a whirlwind will account itself blessed in comparison with your lot after this article appears to-morrow morning," said the editor.

"I am content to abide by the consequences of my act," said Dorlan, quietly.

"Your blood be upon your own head," said the editor. This brought the interview to a close and Dorlan took his departure.

The next morning the following seemingly harmless article from the pen of Dorlan Warthell appeared in the paper whose editor we saw pondering it. It ran as follows:

"In the great crisis of the sixties, the Republican party appeared before the sepulchre of the buried manhood of the Negro race, called it forth from the tomb and divested it of the habiliments of the grave. This portentous achievement shook the earth. The pillars of the Republic tottered but were caught within the titantic grasp of the Republican party, which thereupon made the foundations and superstructure more secure than ever before. As long as the ocean mirrors in her bosom the face of the king of day, just so long shall the hearts of the Negroes cherish the memories of the noble army of men who wrought so nobly for humanity.

"To further the ends so righteously sought a party name was adopted and party machinery created by them. When their tasks were done and they had, for the most part, been gathered to their fathers, other leaders arose and began to operate under this same name and with this same machinery. The charge has often been made that we bestow upon these instruments of our salvation the same devotion that we yielded to the creators and original wielders of the instruments. It is said that we blindly follow the party name regardless of those wielding it and the use to which it is put. The charge may be illustrated by the following comparison :

"A noble man does a cripple a kindness. The man dies and a thrifty neighbor comes into possession of the shoes, clothes and hat that he wore at the time of helping the cripple. The neighbor puts on the leavings of the dead man, appears before the cripple and demands his allegiance because of the clothes worn. The cripple yields the devo-

tion asked for, giving evidence that he was ready
to consider the dead man and the clothes as one
and inseparable. We are charged with acting like
unto this cripple, in the matter of rendering devotion to the party name and machinery, the clothes
left behind by the men who did the actual work of
liberating us.

"In the past we have had no suitable opportunity to clear by an overt act our skirts of the charge
which has been exceedingly damaging to our reputation for intelligence; for the policies of the party
have been mainly good. But unforeseen circumstances have brought us face to face with the golden
opportunity of proving that the picture is over-
drawn, that we have not riveted political chains
upon ourselves, to take the place of the actual
chains torn from us at so fearful a cost. While
adding to our own good name we can also do the
cause of humanity untold good.

"The Spanish-American war has brought us into
contact with many million Filipinos. We must
decide what are to be our relations with them.
Shall we or shall we not deal with them on the
principle that they are and shall ever be regarded as
our equals, is the burning question with the American people. The party with which we have hitherto affiliated, claims to be so busily engaged with
our present duties on the Islands that they must
postpone consideration as to the final status of the

people thereof. The Negroes can favor only one solution of the problem, the recognition of the fact that all men are created equal. They should favor no postponement of a decision, having themselves suffered from a postponement that lasted from midnight of July 4th, 1776, until January 1st, 1863, the time that elapsed between the promulgation of the declaration that all men are created equal, and the application of that declaration to the American slave.

"In view of the silence of the Republican party upon the question of the ultimate status of the Filipinos, it has been decided to organize a party that will spurn silence, that will insist that 'Old Glory' shall continue to float over human beings that can look each other in the face and shout 'We are all equals; no man among us is, in any sense, less free than another.'

"All American citizens willing to consecrate their political efforts to the attainment of this end are invited to elect delegates to be present at Sinclair Hall on the fifteenth of the incoming month. The Negroes having been the chief sufferers from the non-recognition of the principles for which our new party will stand, are expected to take the lead in the new organization.

"Yours for humanity,

"DORLAN WARTHELL."

The manifest purpose of Dorlan to withdraw the Negro vote from the Republicans with the view of forming a new party created a profound sensation. It was discussed by white and colored people, was the theme of conversation in the street cars, hotel corridors, stores, barber shops, saloons, brothels, and on every street corner.

There are in the South, men and women, white and colored, who are endeavoring to meet every issue that arises upon the highest possible plane. The sentiments of such people found expression in the following editorial which accompanied Dorlan's pronunciamento. It ran as follows:

"A Negro has been found to display political independence and moral courage of a high order. He has placed himself in a position where the unthinking will liken him unto the serpent that buried its fangs in the bosom that warmed it. None the less, his act is one of marked heroism. While not endorsing his third party scheme (our party is good enough) we endorse the spirit of initiative and independence that prompts it. We would that this spirit of rebellion against party slavery characterized all the voters of the Southland.

" It is an open secret that the great body of the people of both races in the South are prone to regard elections as nothing more nor less than a perennial struggle for supremacy between the two races. This one issue has been allowed to dwarf all other considerations. Indeed, the South is deaf to all appeals, however urgent, to give consideration to the grave questions arising from time to time affecting the welfare of us all and determining our destiny. Such a condition of isolation from the centers of thought activity is deplorable in the extreme.

"Think of it : by birth a man comes into possession of a full set of political opinions. He is born into a condition of intellectual serfdom ; the mind dares not to wander by a hair's breadth from the narrow estate of thought on which it is born. He who elects to devote his attention to the questions of State must reduce his mentality to the level of the parrot and feel that his life's work will consist in learning to repeat glibly and without alteration whatever party managers may promulgate. What a crime against the human mind whose native air is freedom, to secure which bonfires have been lighted with the thrones of kings !

"What the South needs is a new emancipation. Her giant minds must be allowed to enter the arena of intellectual conflict unfettered, if they are to bring back to the South her departed glory. The Negroes can help to bring about this emancipation. When they cease to vote *en masse ;* when they cease going to the polls as a mark of gratitude to the invaders of the South who now sleep their last sleep and would discountenance, if they could, the perpetuation of race hatred over past issues ; when the sentiment within the Negro race is suffi-

ciently liberal to allow each Negro his manhood
right to record with his vote his own best judgment; when, we say, these desirable conditions obtain among the Negros, we whites will have an
opportunity to escape the scourge with which the
party magnates herd us together even as gratitude
has herded the Negroes.

"With joy we hail the advent of Dorlan Warthell in his new role. May he succeed in inaugu-
rating an era of independent thought among the
Negroes. Let us all hope that we are now behold-
ing a streak of dawn, instead of the trail of a falling star, whose soon fading light will leave our
skies but the darker. Let us hope that the hour is
upon us when the sober torch of reason and not the
withering flames of passion, may guide all of our
voters, white and colored, to the polls."

There are many people in the South who never
read, who never ponder grave questions, but assume
the right to wreak vengeance on the heads of those
who perchance wander from beaten paths in search
of truth. In the above editorial the more enlightened element had spoken; but the unthinking were
also to be heard from.

If Dorlan is depending upon his exalted patriotism, his broad love of humanity, his eager, unself-
ish striving after the good of all—if, we say, he is
depending upon these things to shield him from the

wrath of those whom his act affronted, let him remember that virtue was no shield to Him whose
blood, in the days of yore, anointed the spear of a
Roman soldier upon a hillside on the outskirts of
Jerusalem.

CHAPTER XIV.

BLOODWORTH AT WORK.

The Hon. Hezekiah T. Bloodworth had returned to his home from his interview with Dorlan chagrined, dejected, sorely puzzled as to what to do next.

It was being declared on all sides that the day of isolation was over with the United States, and that it was henceforth to be a world power. Instead of simply directing the affairs of the nation, her statesmen would now be called upon to assist in shaping the destinies of the peoples of the whole earth.

Bloodworth had been cherishing the fond hope that he would be one of the first of American statesmen that would leap into world prominence. His bosom heaved as he thought of the day when his speeches would be read by the inhabitants of all lands and his name would be a household word unto the uttermost parts of the earth. He had unlimited faith in Dorlan's ability and felt that Dorlan could rise equal to the emergency and furnish him the brain power for his widened responsibilities. At the very moment when he felt the need of Dorlan the keenest in all his life, Dorlan refuses to be his mentor.

Bloodworth wept. His tears were not Alexandrian tears of regret that there were no more worlds to conquer, but Bloodworthian tears shed because he could neither borrow nor buy the brains necessary to conquer a world that had come within his reach.

"Hezzy, dear, what on earth troubles you?" asked Mrs. Bloodworth of her perturbed husband.

"My ancestors, confound them," roughly responded Bloodworth.

"He is going crazy," thought Mrs. Bloodworth. "How do your ancestors trouble you, Hezzy?" further queried Mrs. Bloodworth.

"They have handed down to me no brains," roared Bloodworth.

"There, I thought it was brain trouble," thought Mrs. Bloodworth.

"Oh, dear, you have brains," said his wife.

"So has a rabbit. Let me alone, now."

This colloquy had taken place at the dinner table where Bloodworth was voraciously devouring food, in an effort, it would appear, to be strong abdominally if not intellectually. His grief over his plight had not yet affected his appetite. When nearly through the meal a telegram was handed him. It was from the Speakers' Bureau and read thus:

" *Hon. Hezekiah T. Butterworth:*

"Your services are badly needed in the pivotal States. Campaign a flat failure without your lucid speeches. Delay no longer. Report at headquarters at once. The aftermath."

Bloodworth had been given the assurance of a Cabinet portfolio in case his party succeeded. The words, "The aftermath," in the telegram were intended to call attention tò the fact that his preferment was contingent upon his campaign labors. He arose from the table in such an abrupt manner that he upset it, much to the horror of Mrs. Bloodworth.

"Do you wish to send a return message?" asked the messenger boy.

"Tell the Speakers' Bureau and the pivotal States to go to the habitation of the accursed," exclaimed Bloodworth, trudging about the floor, holding the open telegram in both hands as though it was a heavy load.

The messenger boy backed out of the room and hurried away, glad to get out of the presence of the enraged Bloodworth.

"Confound it; I will not be ruined thus" said Bloodworth. Grasping his hat he hurried out of his house to the market. He soon returned and, thrusting a package down on a table in his kitchen, said, "Cook, feed me on fish at every meal. Get the very best fish. Here are some good ones. Begin at supper time. Fish is good for brain food, they say, and I need brains!"

Bloodworth dieted himself on fish for a few days and then began the preparation of the speech with which he was to open his campaign tour in the pivotal states. After great labor the speech was at last finished, and Congressman Bloodworth invited a few intimate friends to hear him deliver it to them in private.

"Friends," said he to the select audience, "of late my mind (meaning Dorlan Warthell) has been a little erratic. It will not serve me as it once did. I have called you here to ask you to tell me whether much of its vigor has departed. If there is too great a gap between my past efforts and my present one, I shall retire from public life. Remember, gentlemen, how much depends on your decision, and be frank with me." Congressman Bloodworth then began his speech. With great effort his hearers refrained from laughter as they listened to what they thought was the most bunglesome address that ever came from the lips of a public servant in a civilized land.

"Mr. Bloodworth, for Heaven's sake, do not take the stump in this campaign. You will be the butt of ridicule of the entire nation." Such was the verdict rendered by one and acquiesced in by the others after listening to the speech.

Bloodworth now completely collapsed. "Gentlemen," he said between his sobs, "take me to my room. I am ill. I knew that a breakdown was due to a man who has worked as hard for his

country as I have. Take me to my room, gentlemen."

Bloodworth was borne to his room and put to
bed. He then dictated a telegram to the Speakers' Bureau, informing them of his illness and consequent inability to participate in the campaign.

The Hon. Hezekiah T. Bloodworth was removed
to the city of R——. to a private sanitarium in order, he said, that he might receive the best medical
attention. Each day he would lay abed feigning
that he was sick. The doctors were unable to tell
what was troubling their patient, but were quite
content to have him remain with them, so hand-
somely were they being paid. Bulletins as to the
state of his health were sent over the country
daily.

Bloodworth succeeded in bribing his night
nurses. With their collusion he was able to escape from the sanitarium each night, returning
just before daybreak in the morning. These
nights were spent by him in the lowest parts of
the city, in gambling dens patronized by the Negroes. He had become aware of the great up-
heaval among the Negroes against Dorlan and he
had decided that the time was auspicious for the
murder. His midnight orgies enabled him to secure tools for his work.

CHAPTRE XV.

HARRY BECOMES A TOOL.

The excitement among the Negroes was so very great that Dorlan decided that something ought to be done to allay it, to the end that the convention which he had called might find a more congenial atmosphere. He issued a call for a public mass meeting, hoping at that meeting to put himself in a better light before the people.

Congressman Bloodworth heard of this proposed mass meeting and chose it as the occasion on which to put an end to Dorlan's life. In his rounds by night he had heard how that Harry Dalton, a ward chairman of the Republican party, was extremely bitter in his feelings toward Dorlan. One night he called at Harry's residence. Morlene met him at the door and his countenance fell. He had not expected to find such intelligence as Morlene's face indicated in a home where dwelled a man as rancorous as Harry had been represented to be. Morlene invited him in. When he saw Harry his spirits rose. His first glance impressed him that Harry could be used as a tool.

Morlene intuitively read sinister purposes in Bloodworth's face. He avoided her searching gaze as much as possible.

"May I have a private interview with you?" asked Bloodworth of Harry.

"Certainly, certainly," said Harry, rising and leading the way to an adjoining room, closing the door behind them. They took seats, Bloodworth putting his chair near to Harry.

"I have come to see you on an important matter," said Bloodworth. "But before I begin I have one question to ask you," he continued. Pausing, and looking directly into Harry's eyes, he asked, "Are you a Republican?"

An angry flush passed over Harry's face. "You insult me, sir, to come into my house to ask me if I am a Republican. I was born a Republican and will die one."

"Don't talk so loud," said Bloodworth, glancing uneasily toward the door, where he thought Morlene might be listening.

"Well, you must not insult me, sir. My color ought to tell you what I am."

"Yes, yes," said Bloodworth, in a sad tone. "There was a time when all colored men were true blue Republicans, but that day is past. A man right here in your ward has gone astray."

"Don't you compare me with that infernal scoundrel, Dorlan Warthell. He claims to be an educated man, and has deserted the Republican party. I could tear his liver out and show it to him, that I could."

"I have come to talk to you about him."

"If you have got any good to say of him, it's no use for you to begin. But if you can tell of any way to get rid of the scoundrel, I am with you."

"Let me tell you my history," said Bloodworth.

Bloodworth now assumed a piteous tone and began: "I am a Southern man. Before the war my father was rich, but would never own a slave, though he lived right in the South.

"When the war broke out, we turned our back on the South and joined the Union Army. That is, my two brothers did. I stayed at home to care for my aged parents.

"When the war was over, the Negroes needed leaders. I decided to lead them. This made all of the Southern white people mad at me, and they called me a scalawag. But I led them just the same, and held office so that the Negroes could say that a Republican was in office. I wanted to go higher. I found a colored boy who was poor but brainy. I gave him all the money I made from politics in return for his help to me. He worked along with me until he had gotten thousands of dollars. Then he left me. He left me just when the Republican party needed him most." Here Bloodworth managed to slip an onion near his eyes and tears appeared.

Harry was deeply moved at this show of emotion. He groaned audibly over the perfidy of the Negro who deserted so true a Republican.

"Yes, Harry," sobbed Bloodworth, "he deserted the party of Lincoln, the party that made his people free, the party that made it possible for you all to be what you are. He deserted me, his true and tried friend. He deserted his own race. Dorlan Warthell is that man."

Harry was now moved to tears—tears of sympathy, tears of shame over the nefarious deed of a colored man, tears of rage.

"I am a Christian," said Harry. "I am a deacon of a church. But I swear by high heaven that no such scoundrel shall be allowed to live! I shall kill him!"

"Nobly spoken! Nobly spoken!" said Bloodworth, grasping Harry's hand warmly. "I am proud that I—that is, that my brothers shed their blood to give freedom to such noble men as you. I am not afraid for the future of your race while such men as you are living."

Harry was grateful to the center of his heart for this tribute to his worth. "May I ever prove worthy of your kind words," said Harry.

"I have no doubt of that. The man who takes Dorlan Warthell out of the way will do enough good to make up for any shortcomings that he might have. I have a well arranged plan for his murder and was only looking for a man worthy of the role of principal actor. Lo, I have found him!"

Bloodworth now unfolded the details of his plot to Harry, and explained to him the part that the latter was to take in the killing.

Morlene, who had listened at the keyhole, had heard in great agony the plottings against the life of Dorlan Warthell. She had no qualms of conscience about listening, for, having seen crime stamped on Bloodworth's face, she had employed the usual method of entrapping criminals—spying.

Bloodworth and Harry were fully determined upon Dorlan's murder. Morlene determined to save his life, even if in so doing she lost her own.

CHAPTER XVI.

A WOMAN AROUSED.

Morlene fully realized the gravity as well as the delicacy of the situation that confronted her. A murder was being planned, the intended victim being an innocent man and one for whom she entertained the greatest possible respect; while the man chosen to strike the fatal blow was none other than her own husband. Her first impulse was to confront Harry, but sober second thought caused her to abandon this purpose, for she remembered that Harry was headstrong; that he never abandoned anything that he had firmly resolved upon doing. She saw that confronting Harry would only have the effect of causing him to lay his plans the deeper and perhaps so far away that she could not by any means intercept them.

Morlene began to consider the advisability of putting in motion a counter current of sentiment in favor of granting the individual citizen the right of independent action, hoping to create such a broad spirit of tolerance that the party or parties who were to use Harry as a tool would be afraid to carry out their programme of murder.

While Harry and Morlene were sitting at the breakfast table one morning, she said to him,

(111)

"Harry, I have come across a very good campaign book and would like to act as agent for it during the next few days. Do you object?"

Without looking up Harry replied, "Of course, not," and continued in meditation of what he regarded as Dorlan's traitorous crime. Every now and then he would lay down his knife and fork and rest his hands on the table, his eyes downcast, so thoroughly was he aroused over Dorlan's presumption in claiming the right to find fault with the Republican party.

When Harry had gone to his work, Morlene took her canvassing outfit and began her labors. She chose with much deliberation the parties to whom she went to sell the book. Her first task upon meeting the party was to set forth the claims of the book. She never failed in effecting a sale, for the parties accosted were willing to pay the price of the book for the privilege of being brought into contact with a woman of such remarkable beauty. They could hardly listen to her recital of the claims of the book for stealing glances at her well shaped, queenly poised head, her pleading, thrilling eyes, her beautiful face, her perfect form. They sought by prolonging the conversation to detain her in their presence as long as possible.

When through talking of her book, Morlene invariably brought up the "Warthell movement" in order that she might discover the temper of the people and find out just how much hope there was of arousing public interest in the matter of securing Dorlan's immunity from attack because he had essayed to pursue an independent course.

A very eminent lawyer, the real head of the Democratic party of the State, expressed himself thus to Morlene:

"To be frank with you, Mrs. Dalton, the fact that the "Warthell movement" might in the end break the solidarity of the negro vote and cause a fraction of that vote to eventually drift to us, has no charms for the Democratic party. For several reasons we do not desire, at present, a contingent of Negro voters. First of all, the coming of the Negro into our ranks will cause our party to disintegrate, many men now being held in it because they there escape contact with the Negro. In the second place, the Anglo-Saxon habit of thought and the Negro habit of thought are so essentially different that we prefer their separation."

"Please explain yourself," requested Morlene.

"Certainly," said the lawyer, not at all weary of the pleasure of looking at and talking to the beauty. "Let me cite you to a Bible incident," he resumed.

"When Peter, in preaching to the Jews, set forth that God had raised Jesus Christ from the dead, and had bestowed upon Him greater power and glory than He had before possessed, the assertion proved to be a befitting climax to a sermon which resulted in the conversion of some three thousand persons.   Paul, in closing a sermon to the Greeks at Athens, alluded to this same resurrection of the dead.   Instead of proving to be the effective climax that it was when Peter was preaching to the Jews, it operated as the weakest point in the discourse, for we are told that at that point, 'some mocked,' and the assemblage postponed the hearing.   Paul in summing up the difference between the Jew and the Greek habit of thought, remarked that the Jews require a sign, and the Greeks seek after wisdom.   You note that the very thing that appealed most strongly to the mind of the Jew—the miraculous raising of the Jesus—was the most repellant to the Greek, who, in his search for wisdom, demanded to know the how of every assertion.

"Returning to the Anglo-Saxon and the Negro—I think I can name a number of differences in their mental attitudes:

"1. The Negro's talent is largely acquisitive; that of the Anglo-Saxon, inquisitive.

"2. The Negro is of a restful temperament; the Anglo-Saxon is characterized by a 'restless discontented, striving, burning energy.'   As a result the Negro is painfully conservative, while the Anglo-Saxon is daringly progressive.

"3. The Negro deals with the immediate; the Anglo-Saxon has a keen eye for the remote,

"4. The Negro is prone to accept statements that lay claim to being postulates; the Anglo-Saxon is skeptical, examining into the foundation of things.

"5. The Negro is impulsive, and is led to act largely by an immediately exciting stimulus, causing the net results of his labors to appear as a series of fits and jerks; the Anglo-Saxon is deliberate, cautious without stagnation, wary and persistent, and his history reveals an unbroken tendency in a given direction.

"6. Hitherto the preponderating tendency of the Negro has been toward disintegration, showing the lack of a proper measure of fellow-feeling; the tendency of the Anglo-Saxon is toward racial integration.

"7. The Negro proceeds by analogies; the Anglo-Saxon by logic.

"8. The Anglo-Saxon is fond of serious discussion and you reach him best through the sublime; the Negro is inordinately fond of joking and you get closest to him through the ludicrous. I do not pretend to say that these are hard and fast lines, separating the Anglo-Saxon and Negro minds into distinct classes, but they indicate a general unlikeness in many particulars.

"Now, we Democrats know how to reach Anglo-Saxon minds and the process is congenial to our general habit of thought. When we address Negroes, we really have to readjust our faculties of approach. Public speakers find that various sections of the same country present this difference, even when all of the people are of the same race. How much greater must be the chasm between two such widely diverging races."

Morlene exhibited no signs of abating interest, so the lawyer proceeded further with his remarks.

"Two other reasons may be given why we prefer to be rid of the Negro," he continued. "The mass of Negroes are poor, some of them very poor, and we have men among us who would not scruple at perpetually bribing these poor by little acts of kindness. A poverty stricken, oppressed, helpless people are comparatively easy prey for the well to do element of an opposite race. In national politics the Negro's devotion to the Republican party exempts him from the chicanery of designing whites who would debauch the suffrage. We do not desire the ignorant Negro vote in municipal affairs for the same reason that the nations of Europe oppose the dismembernent of Turkey. The struggle for possession would be too fierce and demoralizing among the parties desiring the furtherance of their interests. The other reason for not wanting the Negro vote is that the respective traditions of the two races are so essentially different.

"You see they (the Negroes) revere Lincoln, Sumner, Whittier, Lovejoy, Harriet Beecher Stowe, Frederick Douglass, Grant, John Brown, etc. We have no peculiar fondness for these characters. Jefferson Davis, R. E. Lee, Stonewall Jackson, Pickett, Albert Sidney Johnson, etc., are the objects of our love and enthusiasm. You see, it is quite natural that people having such widely differing sentiments should in a measure live apart."

Morlene saw clearly that there was no hope of arousing in this man enthusiasm over Dorlan's work of altering the existing status in matters political. She now departed, the lines of sadness deepening on her face. The lawyer followed her to the door, bade her a polite adieu and turned away, somehow full of the thought that he had conversed with a superior creature.

Morlene next went to the head of the Democratic "machine." He was the man chosen to do the work of "counting out" the opposition if the occasion seemed to require it. He readily purchased a book, and, when called upon, expressed his opinion as to the "Warthell movement."

"To tell the truth, we do not want that fellow to succeed. We hold our people in line by threatening them with the bludgeon of mass voting and Negro domination. The white people let us machine fellows have our own way and will scarcely fight us under any consideration for fear that in destroying the evil that we may represent, they might fall upon another that is worse, namely, "nigger rule," as they call it. Of course, then, we machine fellows don't want any such times as that fellow is trying to inaugurate."

Morlene found the white Republican machine equally antagonistic to Dorlan. They feared that the abandonment of the Republican party by the great mass of Negroes of the South would cause a great influx of Southern whites, which would mean that the day of the small man was over ; for many of the white men who were giants among the Negroes, simply because of their white faces and professed sympathy, would appear to be only pigmies when brought into contact with the abler sections of the whites.

The Negro politicians of the smaller calibre that affiliated with the machine viewed Dorlan's actions with contempt. Their interest in political campaigns ended with ward meetings, county, district, State and national conventions. Whatever profit a campaign was to bring to them personally, they labored to secure while conventions were being held, for they knew that they would be no more an important factor until the time arrived for another series of conventions. Not seeing where Dorlan was to profit personally by his course, they took him to be an enthusiastic crank of some sort. "How much is there in it," was the shibboleth of their creed, learned in the school of "peanut" politics where they operated.

Morlene found many intelligent white and colored men who held views directly opposite to those cited, but they almost invariably wound up by saying, "But Warthell, it turns out, is ahead of his day. Conditions in the South are such that good men of both races are better off out of politics." They were averse to taking any active part in the matter, fearing that, in view of the inflamed state of the public mind, other interests of theirs might be jeopardized.

Finding that all hope of enlisting public sentiment in Dorlan's favor had to be abandoned, Morlene, with a heavy burden on her heart, now turned in the direction of police headquarters. The chief was out, but a subordinate presented himself and desired to know her business.

"Sir," said she, "there is a plan on foot to assassinate Dorlan Warthell, a highly respected Negro of this city."

An angry look came into the face of the policeman. Morlene felt encouraged by this, hoping that she was at last in a place where Dorlan had a friend. She now gave the officer the plans of the conspirators as she had overheard them, taking pains to emphasize the fact that Harry, her husband, was but a weakling in the hands of the chief conspirator, and that she desired that he be wrested from his grasp.

The officer took a memorandum of what Morlene had said. When Morlene had gotten some distance away she recollected something that she

deemed it advisable to tell. She retraced her steps
to headquarters, and, as she drew near the office
door, heard Warthell's name called by the officer with whom she had conferred. Her heart
seemed to cease to beat as she heard this officer
say, "Yes, I hope they will kill the scoundrel. I
believe in every man being true to his race. I call
a Negro who will work against the Republicans
lower than the dogs. I call a Southern white man
who will work against the Democrats as even
lower still. Yes, I hope they will kill the scoundrel.
Let every man stay with his own race, by gosh."

Morlene turned away trembling in every fibre.
When she had proceeded some distance she turned,
and pointing her finger in the direction of the
building from which she had just come, said,
"Ah! justice, justice, whither art thou fled? Red-
handed murder now sits in thy temple and occupies
thy throne! How long wilst thou withhold thy
presence from this beautiful, but blighted Southland?" Passers by did not know what to make of
this beautiful woman standing with outstretched
hand, a look of sorrow and lofty scorn upon her
face.

CHAPTER XVII.

CLANDESTINELY, YET IN HONOR.

Returning to her home, Morlene sent the following note to Dorlan :

"MR. DORLAN WARTHELL :

"DEAR SIR—I have come into possession of information that renders an interview with you imperative. For reasons that are entirely satisfactory to my conscience, I desire that the interview be private. I assure you that nothing but the most *desperate* circumstances could influence me to take this step. Upon the peril of your life meet me at the end of the Broad Street car line promptly at eight o'clock.

"THE ARDENT EXPANSIONIST."

A few minutes before the appointed hour, Dorlan was at the place designated. A thickly-veiled lady stepped off of the eight o'clock car and her shapeliness told Dorlan that it was Morlene. The two walked onward together until they were at such a distance as not to encounter inquisitive passers-by.

"Mr. Warthell," began Morlene, "my first task is to impart to you certain information. There exists a conspiracy, the object of which is to effect your murder at the mass meeting which you are to hold."

"Nothing that happens in the South any longer excites surprise in me," said Dorlan, no trace of emotion in his voice. Not a muscle of his noble face twitched at the news.

Morlene resumed: "I have further to say, that the state of the public mind toward you is such as is calculated to encourage rather than to destroy criminal intentions directed against you. Enlightened or unenlightened, the forces in favor of the existing order of things regard you as a disturbing factor in the body politic. Your position is peculiarly dangerous in that the weaker minds will grow to regard your murder as a civic duty."

"No one can gainsay the elements of danger in the situation," said Dorlan.

"The police, I fear, will not furnish you the protection that you need," remarked Morlene.

"Perhaps not," responded Dorlan.

Morlene now threw back her veil and turned her anxious eyes full on Dorlan. "Mr. Warthell," she said, "the cool manner in which you receive the information which I give, indicates that you are not as regardful of your life as might be the case."

Dorlan replied: "My life has no charms for me, *per se*. I am wedded to certain purposes for which I have learned to live. I will gladly yield my life for their furtherance at any time that result can be achieved. If the ends for which I strive are found to be unattainable, life has no further interest for me."

"Mr. Warthell, the world needs your services," said Morlene in earnest tones.

"It may be that the world has a greater need for my death. I am enough of a fatalist to believe that whatever the world needs it gets. Note how opportune have been the great births and deaths of history," replied Dorlan.

"Mr. Warthell, I have not come here to theorize on the comparative value of life and death. I have come to save your life. Have you any relatives living?"

"None," said Dorlan.

"Oh, that there was a mother or a sister to make the plea that I must make!" said Morlene, sorrowfully. "Wait," she said, as though a new idea had struck her. "Mr. Warthell, is there not somewhere in the world a noble girl whose heart you have won and who has accepted you as the companion by whose side she is to journey through life?"

"My life has not been altogether without love," said Dorlan, a trace of emotion appearing in his voice. "But it was a boyish love. The little girl fell asleep in her twelfth summer. Were she alive to-night there might be something to chain me to life. As it is my personal life is barren of inducements and I am free to offer myself upon the altar for the good of my country."

Morlene dropped upon her knees; tears had made their appearance in her eyes. With clasped hands and face upraised to his, she said: "Mr. Warthell,

I beg of you, spare your life.   Spare me the horror
of knowing that you were foully murdered.   You
have no mother, no sister, no lover.   I am only a
stranger to you.   Argument fails me and I can
only plead."

Dorlan turned away, unable to look into that
sweet, sorrowful face and say it nay   "It is best
that I die," said Dorlan to himself.   "If I lived I
could not escape falling in love with this divine
being."   To Morlene he remarked, his head still
averted, "Sweet is your voice and earnest your
pleadings. Think it not ungallant in me to say
that the stern voice of duty engrosses my ear and
I obey its summons.   If I die at my post of duty
you will be one to revere my memory."

Morlene arose and moved around so as to be face
to face with Dorlan who was seeking to avoid her
gaze. "Answer one question for me, Mr. Warthell.
Is there anything connected with your life that
causes you to think that death would be a
personal gain to you as well as a gain to your
country? I do not ask out of curiosity, you must
know.   It behooves me to know all the factors to
be reckoned with in my attempt to save your life."

"No personal considerations would induce me to
seek to destroy my life. Let that information suf-
fice," said Dorlan.

The very suppression manifest in Dorlan's reply
and tone of voice revealed to Morlene that the full

answer to her query was "Yes." She now ceased her pleading. She saw that the labor of saving Dorlan's life was more largely upon her than she had at first supposed. She had even his indifference to life to combat. Undaunted by this fresh complication she girded her spirit for the conflict.

In silence the two went toward the place where Morlene was to board the car to return to her home. When they arrived at the place of parting, Morlene said, "Remember, I say, you shall not die." Dorlan looked at her, smiled sadly, turned and walked away.

CHAPTER XVIII.

WHO WINS?

The night of the mass meeting came at last, and there was a tremendous outpouring of the Negroes, recruited mainly from the ranks of the toiling masses. Scattered here and there in the audience were a few of the educated Negroes, drawn to the meeting to see how Dorlan was to fare in his attempt to breast the current of Negro loyalty to the Republican party. The women in the audience outnumbered the men, a fact not to be wondered at, when it is known that the Negro women of the South are, perhaps, the most ardent and unyielding Republicans in the whole length and breadth of the land. Closely veiled, Morlene sat in the audience, the embodiment of anxiety. The moment for the supreme contest between herself on the one hand and Bloodworth and Harry on the other, for the life of Dorlan, was drawing frightfully near.

At the appointed hour Dorlan entered the building from the rear door, walked across the platform and took his seat. Somehow the world expects the body of a man to give some indication of the soul within, wherefore all pictures of Satan represent him as being ugly. Those who came to the meeting hating Dorlan felt a more kindly feeling creeping into their consciousness as they saw that heaven had thought kindly enough of him to grant unto him the form of a prince, an intellectual brow, a truly handsome face that wore a look of earnest, honest purpose.

As Dorlan scanned the audience his heart swelled with joy at its immense proportions. Wrong though they sometimes were, Dorlan had the most profound faith in the good intentions of the Negro masses. He held that the intentions of no people on earth were better, and that the sole need of the Negroes was proper light.

Dorlan's analysis of the situation was as follows: The feeling encountered was largely a religious one. The Negroes believed unqualifiedly in the direct interposition of God in the affairs of men. They believed in the personality, activity and insidiousness of the Devil. They believed that God had specifically created the Republican party to bring about their emancipation. On the other hand they regarded the Democratic party as the earthly abode of the devil, created specifically and solely for the purpose of harassing them. Thus, whoever opposed the Republican party was sinning against God; and whoever voted against that party was in league with the devil.

Such were the views held by the less enlightened, Dorlan felt. In order to meet the situation he had prepared a speech that traced from a human point of view the development of the two parties. Once disabuse their minds of the direct, specific heavenly origin of the Republican party, and the way would be open to show, that as men made it, men could improve upon its policies. So at the appointed hour he arose and began his speech. It riveted the attention of his hearers, and they listened with eager ears to Dorlan's recital of the workings of the forces and counter forces that brought about their emancipation. Freedom had burst upon them so suddenly, was so glorious a boon, that their simple minds readily concluded that it dropped bodily, as it were, from the skies. They were now glad to gain a clear understanding of that phenomenal happening. Their feelings of resentment died away entirely, and they who came to jeer, frequently broke forth into applause.

Dorlan closed his speech with a thrilling peroration, urging the Negroes to gird themselves for the holy task of carrying to the uttermost parts of the earth the doctrine of the inherent, inalienable equality of all men.

Morlene could scarcely repress tears of joy over the happy turn of events. But her joy was to be short lived.

Bloodworth had employed a number of viciously inclined Negroes to put out the lights, bar the doors and foment excitement. In the midst of the disturbance Harry was to effect the murder of Dorlan. Bigoted Harry had not been in the least affected, nor were his mercenary compatriots in any wise moved, by Dorlan's utterances. When the speech was finished, at a given signal the lights were extinguished and a tumult raised.

Harry had closely noted the position of Dorlan on the platform, and as soon as the lights were out began to make his way toward him. As there was no one on the platform but Dorlan, he did not fear making a mistake as to the man he was to assault.

Morlene had employed a young man of strength and courage to sit by and keep close watch on Harry to thwart any attempts he might make. As Harry made his way with eager cat-like tread, he was followed by the young man appointed to watch him. When near Dorlan, Harry drew his pistol but felt it wrenched from his hand by some one of superior strength. Discovering that he was followed, Harry turned and sought to mingle with the crowd in the hope of eluding his pursuer. In this he was successful.

Morlene, thickly veiled, had been sitting in a corner of the auditorium throughout the meeting. In a satchel she had brought along a small lighted lantern. She knew the building well, and even in the midst of the hubbub and excitement incident to the putting out of the lights, had made her way to the platform where-

on was Dorlan. Now handling her lantern so
that it guided her directly to Dorlan, without
informing others of her movements, she crept to
his side. She found him seated, his head bent
forward resting on his hand. Even now his first
thought was of the future of the race, seeking to
keep alive in his bosom to the moment of death,
the hope that it would rise in spite of the unthinking element that now sought his life.

Morlene whispered into his ear, " Mr. Warthell,
do not die here. As a friend, a sincere friend, I
plead with you to live for all our sakes." The
presence of Morlene in such a dangerous situation
thoroughly aroused Dorlan. He sprang to his feet
determined to live until she was out of danger, at
least. " Here is a lantern," said she, handing it to
him.

"Keep close to me," said Dorlan to Morlene.
To the throng he said: "Gentlemen, vacate the
aisle to the extreme right. Whoever obstructs
that pathway to the door, does so at the peril of
his life. I have given fair warning and hold you ac-
countable for whatever results from your failure to
obey. His voice was so commanding and he spoke
with such self-assurance, that the movement to
clear the aisle designated began at once; but the
words had scarcely escaped his lips when he was
stabbed from the rear. Turning upon his assail-
ant, he felled him to the floor with a powerful
blow. Flashing the light across the face of the

fallen man, Dorlan and Morlene both saw that it was Harry.

"My duty is here," said Morlene, as she stooped and took Harry's head upon her lap.

"Good-bye. I must go. I am wounded," said Dorlan to Morlene, as he started for the door.

Morlene assured herself that Harry was not seriously hurt, and administered restoratives which she had been thoughtful enough to bring along. She was the while experiencing anxious thoughts as to the dangerousness of Dorlan's wound. At the earliest possible moment Morlene left Harry, (who was now reviving) and went to telephone for the ambulance. It came and, with the aid of lanterns, following a trail of blood, they came upon Dorlan, unconscious, the wondering stars peeping down upon his upturned face.

*   *   *   *   *   *

Morlene reached home on that eventful night some time before Harry. After his murderous assault on Dorlan, having recovered from the stunning effects of the blow that had felled him, he had gone from saloon to saloon, drinking and very hilarious over his night's work. At three o'clock in the morning he reached his home in a half-drunken state. Morlene had been anxiously awaiting his coming.

As Harry stepped into the room, one glance at Morlene's face had the effect of somewhat sobering him. Her face, her eyes, her attitude and, when she spoke, her voice, conveyed to the half-drunken Harry her feelings of utter scorn and indignation. He dropped into a chair. His eyes were bleared, his lips slightly ajar and his hands limp at his side, as he looked at the wrathful Morlene.

"Harry Dalton," said she, "You are to all intents and purposes a villainous murderer. I know of your nefarious plottings and I witnessed your cowardly attempt to assassinate Mr. Warthell, a man, the latchet of whose shoes the possessor of a heart like yours is unworthy to unloose. But your intended victim shall not die, unless an evil genius presides over the affairs of men. I have only waited here to tell you how I loathe your crime and that I exhausted every known means to thwart you. Now I leave you!"

Morlene started toward the door through which Harry had just come and which led into the hallway. Harry, who had taken a seat not far from the door, arose as if to intercept her.

"Stand back from that door, Harry," said Morlene pulling a pistol from her pocket and pointing it at him. Morlene had been careful to see that every chamber of the pistol was empty, so that no actual physical harm would result from the drawing of it.

Harry knew that Morlene, when a country girl, had learned to shoot well, and her angry looks made him feel that her knowledge as to how to shoot was supplemented with a determination to shoot if he disobeyed her. Lifting his hands as if imploring her not to shoot, Harry recoiled and Morlene glided out of the room, locking the door behind her.

For some time Harry stood in the floor bewildered by the sudden and most unexpected turn of events. At length he aroused himself and succeeded in breaking out of the room. It was too late, however, to find any trace of Morlene. She had made good her escape.

CHAPTER XIX.

THE SCENE SHIFTS.

An aged Negro woman trudged along Newton Street in the city of Chicago. The ponderous strokes of Father Time had at last bent her form forward, pushing it toward the dust whence it came. She was aided in her shuffling gait by a crooked and knotted walking stick, which she made use of with her left hand. Her attire betokened extreme poverty and was evidently unequal to the task of shielding her from the chilly winds, which sought with zeal every unprotected spot, and whipped the tears from her eyes. In her right hand she carried a small tin box, her bony fingers clasping it as tightly as they could. A shawl was thrown over her head somewhat concealing her features. Strange to say, a close inspection of the woman's face impressed one that there was cheerfulness, even happiness, written thereon, despite her forlorn condition. As she crept along she scanned the buildings closely, evidently trying to locate some particular house.

A young woman standing in the doorway of the Lincoln Hospital, attired in the garb of a sick nurse, saw the old woman drawing near. "The poor soul must be suffering greatly," said the nurse,

(134)

reaching for her pocketbook. She had determined upon emptying its contents into the aged woman's hand as the latter passed by.

Instead of passing, however, the woman stopped a short distance from the nurse. Her frame shivering from cold, her eyes surveyed the entire front of the building in the doorway of which stood the nurse. Seemingly satisfied with the result of her inspection she drew nearer and said: "Leddy, please, miss, is dis de Linktum horsepittul?"

"Yes, aunty, this is the Lincoln Hospital," the nurse replied.

The woman dropped her stick and the tin box and clapped her hands, saying, "Thankee! Thankee Jesus! Thankee! Heah at las'! De ole ship dun foun' er harbur. Got er place ter cross ober Jordun."· Looking at the nurse, she said, "Chile, does yer know anyt'ing 'bout Jesus? Oh! he promis' me dis, an' he's kep' his word." Fumbling in her pocket, she drew out a soiled and crumpled piece of paper. This she handed to the nurse, who found that it entitled the woman to admission into the hospital.

"Come with me," said the nurse in kindly tones.

Gathering up her stick and tin box, she did as she was bidden. The woman was duly registered and assigned to the ward in which this nurse was an attendant.

One afternoon, the nurse sat by the bedside of her new patient humming a tune. The woman almost stopped breathing to listen. Sitting up in her bed, she said to the nurse, "Leddy, ken you fin' a pair ub specks fitten' fur one ob my age?"

"I will try, aunty," replied the nurse.

After a diligent search, the nurse succeeded in finding a pair, wondering as she searched what possible use the woman could have for them. The woman adjusted the spectacles to her eyes and bent her gaze on the nurse.

"Leddy, please sing dat chune ergin," she said.

The nurse did as requested. Before she had proceeded far with the singing, the woman burst forth, "Laws 'a mussy! Ef it ain't Lenie!"

"Aunt Catherine!" exclaimed the nurse, springing to her feet and throwing her arms around the woman's neck.

Aunt Catherine's bedimmed eyesight and impaired hearing had prevented her from discovering before this that her nurse was none other than Morlene. On the other hand, Aunt Catherine's changed appearance was what interfered with Morlene's recognition of her when they first met. When the woman said "Lenie," it was all that was needed, for it was an appellation used in addressing Morlene by Aunt Catherine only.

After many exchanges of tender greetings, Morlene disentangled herself from Aunt Catherine's loving embrace, saying, "Dear Aunt Catherine, do tell me all about yourself since the day I left you to wait on—on—Harry. I searched R—— from one end to the other, time and again, looking for you. And here you are in Chicago! Tell me how you have fared?"

"Chile," said Aunt Catherine, "seein' you, Lenie, hez driv' erway all my trubbuls. 'Pears ter me, I dun got young ergin an' am down Souf at de ole home." After an interval Aunt Catherine proceeded to tell her experiences, not, however, before she had taken the tin box from under her pillow. With that clasped fondly, she began :

"W'en I retched de city arter leavin' de ole homestid, I 'gun ter hunt fur wuck. I got er place ter cook fur er white fambly. De leddy dat hi'ed me wuzunt rich. She wus jes a good liver. Her husban's bizness fell off an' she had ter hire jes' one 'oman ter cook, an' wash, an' i'ne, an' scrub de floors, an' keep house. I wuz de fus' ter try it, but I kudden' hole out, chile. I jes' kudden'. Er sprightly gal tuck my place. Den I hed er hard time, Lenie. Yer Aunt Catharine hed ter beg frnm door ter door. I slep' on bar' floors in shackly houses, dat wuz empty kase folks wouldn't rent 'um. I went to de dumps an' scratched in de trash piles fur charcoals and scraps ter burn ter keep me warm. I begged money ernuf ter cum ter Churcargo, an' heah I is. Dey tole me dat Linktum wuz frum dis State an' I wuz in hopes ub doin' bettah up heah. But, Lenie, 'pears ter me dat de po darky aint got much ub er show enywhurs. I hez found it hard Norf an' Souf."

"Well, henceforth, I shall take charge of you, and walk through life by your side, my dear Aunt Catherine," said Morlene, feelingly.

The woman dropped the tin box, pulled her spectacles down a little and looked over them at Morlene. "Ain't the doctah tole yer yit?" asked Aunt Catherine, in evident surprise.

"Told me what, my dear?" enquired Morlene.

"Why, chile, I aint heah fur long. De doctahs sez I kaint git well. De gospil train dun blowed. It is rollin' into de depot. Capting Jesus is de cunducter. I hez my ticket ready." Aunt Catherine with her broken voice now tried to sing the following lines, swinging to and fro as she sang:

> "De Gospil train am comin',
>   I heah it jes' at han',
> I heah de car wheels movin',
>   Er rumblin' through de lan'.
> Git on bo'd, little chillun,
> Git on bo'd, little chillun,
> Git on bo'd, little chillun,
>   Dare's room fur many mo'."

"Yes, Lenie, I'll soon be on bo'd," resumed Aunt Catherine. "De Yankees was mighty anxious to set us poor darkeys free, but it ain't done me no good. Fack ub de mattah, Lenie, freedum mebbe good fur you young uns who wuzunt use ter de ole times. Fur your sakes I is glad its come. But I'se hed a hard time. Enyhow, it is mos' ober now. Marse Maury is ded, an' Missus is ded, an' a upstart is on de ole place, an' hez been driftin' 'bout frum 'pillar ter pos'.'" Aunt Catherine's mind now ran back to the good old past and a joyful light came into her face. " Do yer see dis tin box?" she asked, breaking her silence.

Morlene nodded affirmatively, not trusting herself to speak, so torn up were her feelings over the account of faithful Aunt Catherine's sufferings.

"Lenie," said she, leaning toward Morlene, a most serious look upon her face, " as yer value yer own soul, do wid dis tin box lack I'm gwine ter tell yer." Aunt Catherine was now speaking in low and solemn tones. " W'en yer wuz er gal, Lenie, did yer ebber heah dat our fust juty on jedgment day would be to git up frum whar eber we wuz burrit and hunt fur de diff'runt pieces ub our finger nails dat we hed cut off all through life?"

"Yes, Aunt Catherine," responded Morlene.

" Wal, dis box hez got all my finger nails dat I cut off since I wuz er gal. Bury dis box at de foot ub Maury and Missus, Lenie. W'en jedgment day comes I want ter git up wid dem. Ef my nails is burrit by dem, I'll have ter go dare whar dey is. See? Yer know white folks ginilly ain't got heartfelt 'ligun like cullud folks. But Marse and Missus shuah got shuah 'nuf 'ligun. I wants ter git up wid 'um an' stan' by 'um in jedgment, ter speak up fur um, ef eny body wants ter go ergin' um jes' kase dey is white. See? Ef dey doan b'long in hebun, den nobody doan." Here Aunt Catherine paused, the talk having nearly exhausted her.

"But, Aunt Catherine," interposed Morlene, "when you do pass away, which I hope will not be soon, let me bury your *whole body* where you tell me to put this tin box. Lemuel Dalton surely would not refuse to allow the fulfillment of the solemn promise made to you by Uncle Maurice and his wife."

"Chile, I hed ter sell dis ole body ter de doctah ter git mony ter lib on while heah."

"Oh, Aunt Catherine!" exclaimed Morlene, holding up her hands in horror.

"Ha, ha, ha!" laughed Aunt Catherine. "That aint so bad, Lenie," she said. "I sole my soul ter Jesus long ergo, an' w'en he takes it, dese doctahs kin do whut dey choose wid my pore ole body." Morlene now burst into tears.

Lovingly Aunt Catherine stroked Morlene's hair with her hand, saying: "Bettah be laughin' fur joy, chile, fur er few more risin's an' settin's ub de sun an' I'll be in glory." Unable to longer endure the contemplation of Aunt Catherine's sufferings and approaching end, Morlene arose and fled to her room.

A few days after the conversation herein recorded Aunt Catherine passed peacefully away. The doctors that had purchased the body presented themselves and laid claim thereto. Morlene told them the story of Aunt Catherine's life of faithful service and subsequent sufferings, and begged the boon of taking the body back to Tennessee for burial.

Her request was refused, however, the physicians deciding that they would not allow a matter of sentiment to stand in the way of advancing the interests of science. Taking the tin box, so solemnly committed to her charge, Morlene turned her face toward Tennessee, journeying thither to fulfill the last request of Aunt Catherine.

For some time Morlene had been pondering a proper course to be pursued toward Harry for the future, and her approaching visit to R—— accentuated the matter. More and more she began to regard him as an unbalanced enthusiast, whose errors, in view of his outlook, were not altogether unnatural. Pity, deep pity, stole into her heart for poor Harry, and she decided, as her train was speeding onward, to return to him in the hope of widening his horizon and giving him a clearer view of what was required of an American citizen. If she would be of service to Harry, her train must move at a faster rate than that at which it is now traveling.

CHAPTER XX.

THE BYSTANDERS CHEER.

From his quest of Morlene, on the morning of her escape, Harry returned to his home in a sullen mood. Morlene's lack of appreciation of his disinterested patriotism which her course revealed to him, was a blow in itself, apart from his loss of her as a wife. The fact that he had lost his wife and had not slept any during the whole night did not, however, cause him to remain away from his accustomed labor that day. Cooking his own breakfast, he ate his solitary meal and went forth to his daily task. Anxious to learn what view others took of the happening of the previous night, he purchased a copy of a morning paper and read its comments thereon. It was the same paper that had commented so favorably upon what it termed the "Warthell Movement." Harry turned immediately to the editorial columns and read far enough to see that his act was being condemned. Thereupon he tore the paper into shreds, threw it to the ground and trampled upon it.

"Sure sign that I did right to attack that scoundrel Warthell, if it has made this old Democratic paper mad. Ha, ha, ha! Morlene thought I was doing wrong. I wasn't though, anybody can see, for what would this old Democratic paper be kicking about if what I did wasn't against it?" Thus muttered Harry to himself as he went on to his work.

"We'll hear a different tune when the Northern Republican papers begin to discuss our attempt to get rid of these Negro traitors who are plotting to undo all that the North has done for us. I take my medicine from the North; let the South go where it please. See? Any Negro that will stand up for the South against the North is an infernal, ungrateful, good for nothing rascal, and *ought* to be killed. Tell him I said so." These last words, addressed by Harry to himself, were accompanied with the shaking of a clenched fist at an imaginary foe. The more he pondered his course, the more he praised himself, and the more outrageous Morlene's desertion of him seemed. Eagerly he awaited the coming of the Northern papers that he might regard his vindication as complete.

Harry went about his daily task in a half cheerful, half moody frame of mind, pondering what steps to take with reference to his wife, but arriving at no definite conclusion.

After the lapse of a day or so the eagerly-looked-for Northern Republican paper came. Harry smiled with satisfaction, saying to himself: "Now we shall hear the thing talked about right."

The article was headed, "A Crime Against Freedom." Harry now thought that the article was going to gibbet Dorlan Warthell for having committed a crime against the freedom of the Negro by refusing to longer affiliate with the party that gave him freedom. He reread the caption, "A Crime Against Freedom." "Yes, yes; only it ought to be 'An Unpardonable Crime,' for that is what it was." Eager to feast on the invectives to be hurled at Dorlan, he stood still on the street corner and began to read:

"The United States of America is a government ruled by the duly ascertained will of a majority of its citizens. Each qualified citizen has the right of casting one vote in support of whatever side of an issue that pleases him. Each citizen has the further right to use all legitimate means in his power to induce other citizens to cast their votes as he casts his.

"The right of advocacy is, if possible, more sacred than the right to vote, for the votes of fellow citizens go well nigh the whole length in shaping a man's environments. Since the votes of others are the majority influence in determining a man's environments, it is manifestly unjust to deny him the opportunity of influencing these votes. He who strikes at freedom of speech strikes at the cornerstone of our republic, and, to our view, commits the greatest crime that a citizen can commit against a government.

"It is well known that we are in full accord with the Republican party's policy with reference to the

Philippine Islands. While we are firmly of the opinion that the party is right, we nevertheless strenuously insist that those who hold contrary views be accorded the right to advocate those views.

" Dorlan Warthell, a Negro in the South, has seen fit to publicly disapprove of a portion of the party's policy, whereupon a Negro Republican zealot has sought to take his life. The Republican party repudiates such vile methods and the man who resorts to them.

" Mr. Warthell has as much right to express his views, whatever they may be, as the President of the nation. The fact that he is a member of a race that obtained its freedom through the instrumentality of the Republican party does not alter the matter in the least. The Republican party has no politcal slaves and desires none. It seeks to commend itself to the hearts and consciences of men, and spurns every semblance of coercion.

" The miscreant who sought to kill Mr. Warthell, because that individual dared to be a man, is unworthy of life. If the arms of justice are too short to reach him, it is hardly to be hoped that he will have the good sense to bring his own unprofitable existence to a close."

When Harry had finished he let the paper fall to the ground. He felt as though the very skies had fallen down upon him. To find the great Republican party lifting its voice in condemnation of his act was more than he could bear. Stooping down, he picked up the paper and re-read the closing paragraph.

"I can surprise them yet. They say ' It is hardly to be hoped that he will have the good sense to bring his own unprofitable existence to a close.' Aha! we shall see!" said Harry, a grim determination settling over his gloomy soul.

Deserted by Morlene, repudiated by the Republican party, which he had always regarded as the vicegerent of God, Harry decided to have his life come to a close in some way. He began to give earnest thought to the finding of the proper method of departure. In the matter of closing his earthly career, he was hampered by his religious views. He was a firm believer in Heaven and in a literal Hell. In common with many other Negroes, he believed that the Bible contained a specific declaration to the effect that all sins could be forgiven a man except the sin of self-murder.

To cause himself to die and yet escape Hell was the problem that now occupied Harry's mind. From day to day he deliberated on the matter. At one time he was attracted by the thought of laying down upon a railroad track in some isolated spot in the hope that he would fall asleep and fail to awake on the approach of a train. In case he did not awake, he thought that his death could properly be construed as an accident. Then he thought of becoming an attendant upon the sick, choosing

such patients to serve as were afflicted with danger-
ons contagious diseases.

Months and months passed, summer and fall
sped by and made way for winter, but Harry's purpose remained. The question of a way to die was
at last solved for him in a most unexpected manner. One afternoon as he was returning from
work, he saw far ahead of him, coming in his direction, a pair of runaway horses hitched to a double
seated carriage. As the carriage came near he saw
that the driver's seat was empty and that a white
lady and three children were seated in the carriage
in imminent peril of their lives. "Thank God!"
Harry murmured, "the way appears." As the
horses came galloping down the street, Harry stationed himself in such a position that he would be
able to make an effort to intercept them.

"Get out of the way, you fool!" frantically
shouted one after another of the bystanders.
"Those horses will kill you." To all of this Harry paid no heed. Harry's sublime heroism stilled
the shoutings of the multitude. The people stood
mute gazing at Harry, so unflinchingly awaiting the
coming of the runaways. When the horses came
sweeping by, Harry leapt to the head of the one
nearest him and grappled the bridle. The maddened horses bore him from his feet and onward,
but Harry clung to the bridle. Unable to longer
carry so heavy a weight clinging to his mouth, the
horse to which Harry was holding checked his speed

and brought his fellow to a stand.   This result was
not achieved, however, without fatal injuries to
Harry.

Turning the bridle loose Harry fell at the feet
of the horses, others now rushing forward to take
charge of them.   As Harry lay upon the ground
covered with dust and blood, a crowd of citizens
gathered about him.   The lady whose life had been
saved, the wife of a leading banker, got out of the
carriage, and, elbowing her way through the crowd,
stooped down to wipe the blood stains from Harry's
face.

Harry who had been unconscious revived and
smiled feebly in recognition of the kindness.   The
crowd that had witnessed his heroic deed now gave
a mighty cheer, joyful that he was alive.   Before
the cheering subsided, the light of life died out of
Harry's eyes and his soul had sped.

CHAPTER XXI.

TO BEGIN LIFE ANEW, AS IT WERE.

When a few hours later Morlene arrived at her home in R——, she found crepe on the door, and was told by a neighbor that was just leaving, that Harry had died that day. She stood as if rooted to the spot, her beautiful eyes recording the storm of pity that was rising in her bosom. Mechanically she turned and placed one foot on the step to the porch, as if to leave. "Horror! Horror! Horror everywhere!" she cried out. "But why am I fleeing? It is abroad in the whole expanse of earth. If Harry *was* to die, tell me, tell me, why he could not have awaited to carry my forgiveness with him." In that moment, looking back upon her whole career since the death of Maurice Dalton, she felt her faith in the benevolent character of the arbiter of human destinies rudely shaken. Her body recoiled in response to a like impulse of her soul that shrank from the benumbing misanthropism that sought to lay its cold dead fingers on her heart. In one last supreme effort to retain her faith she burst forth into song. In tones angelic, from a heaving bosom, she poured forth the following words:

"Abide with me! Fast falls the eventide;
The darkness deepens—Lord, with me abide!
When other helpers fail, and comforts flee,
Help of the helpless,—O abide with me!"

(149)

When Morlene began to sing her eyes glistened with tears; but these now disappeared as a look of submission stole therein. Again humbly obedient to the forces that were guiding her life, she entered her home, knelt and gazed long at the features of Harry, her spirit seeking to unravel that mystic smile that his face was wearing even in death.

*　　*　　*　　*　　*　　*

Two days later the business men of R—— swore, the housewives grew red in the face, but it was all of no avail. The Negro laboring men and cooks were determined upon going to Harry's funeral, even if it cost them their jobs. So, business was partially paralyzed and the white women of fashionable circles had to enter their own kitchens while the Negroes thronged to the church wherein the funeral services were to be held.

Though the funeral was to take place at two o'clock, the edifice was crowded at twelve, those anxious for seats rushing there thus early. According to the custom of the church to which Harry belonged, his body had lain therein all the night previous and his brethren and sisters of the church had assembled and conducted a song and prayer service over his remains. When the hour for the funeral arrived, the pulpit was full of ministers of various denominations.

Harry had, according to the custom prevailing, chosen the hymns to be sung at his funeral, the text

from which the funeral sermon was to be preached,
the ministers who were to officiate—in fact, had arranged for every detail of the occasion. Everything was done according to his wishes.

The services were at last brought to a close and
the funeral procession was formed. The hearse
led the way being followed by the great concourse
of the members of the church, walking *en masse*
and chanting mournful dirges as they proceeded.
Following the throng came the carriage containing Morlene and Stephen Dalton, Harry's father.
The old man's form is now bent, his short hair
white and he is sad at heart that it is Harry's funeral and not his own. Following this carriage
containing Morlene and Stephen Dalton was that
of the banker, who with his wife and children had
come to pay this tribute of respect to the memory
of Harry. When the procession reached the cemetery, twilight had come to render the interment
peculiarly solemn.

Harry was lowered to his last resting place and
each one of his immediate friends picked up a clod
and cast it into the open grave, the good-bye salutation for the dead. All staid until the grave was
covered over, then turned to leave.

The cemetery in which Harry had been laid to
rest was upon an elevation. When the carriage
containing Morlene had proceeded homeward for
some distance and was at the point where the
slowly declining elevation had reached a level

with the lower lands, she caused the driver to stop for a few minutes while she and Stephen Dalton alighted. The two stood and looked for awhile in silence toward the cemetery above them, the lighted lamps burning dimly among the trees up there. One solitary star peered out of the eastern sky. Its lonely light, like words spoken in the hour of grief, evidently sought to cheer, but only served to make the feeling of sadness deepen.

By and by in tones soft and low and earnest, Morlene broke the silence, saying: "Father, Harry's body lies up yonder, and, behold, the place is lighted. May we not hope that his spirit, in spite of his weaknesses, has gone *upward*, and may we not also hope that there the spirit, too, has light, more light than came to it in this darkened world?" Stephen Dalton made no reply. The only thing that he now cared to answer was the final summons. He regarded himself as an alien on earth. The two re-entered the carriage and drove to the city.

The next day, Morlene repaired to the Dalton estate and buried at the designated spot the box that Aunt Catherine had entrusted to her care. Thus came to a close one epoch in Morlene's life.

CHAPTER XXII.

We left Dorlan sorely wounded on the night of the mass meeting. Though he was immediately furnished with the best available medical attention, it did not prevent the setting in of a species of blood poisoning which rendered his condition peculiarly precarious. As soon as it was deemed advisable, he was carried North and placed under the care of an eminent specialist.

Dorlan began to slowly improve, but at such a rate that he now saw that he was to be a mere onlooker to the presidential campaign in which he had hoped to be the determining factor. On the day of the election his interest was so great that he got out of bed and sat at his window, eagerly scanning the faces of the voters as they went, and came from the polls, hoping, it seemed, to tell from their countenances what verdicts they were rendering. He had made arrangements with a newsboy to bring him a copy of the first "Extra" to be issued giving information as to how the conflict had terminated.

At a comparatively early hour of the night the newsboy knocked on Dorlan's door. "Come in," called out Dorlan. The boy poked his head in the door, cast a quick glance about, then entered. "Here's your paper, Mister. Good news for *you*," said he, smiling as he handed the paper to Dorlan.

"How do you know that it contains news pleasing to me?" inquired Dorlan, looking at the boy earnestly.

"'Cause you are a colored man," responded the boy, with an air of complete assurance. Having been paid, he now hurried out to proceed on his route.

"Even the children feel that they know the politics of every Negro by glancing at his skin. Too bad! I suppose the boy means to say the Republicans have won," mused Dorlan. He now looked at his paper and soon was convinced that the Republicans had won an overwhelming victory.

Dorlan was stunned. "What!" he exclaimed, "Has a reaction against that idealism which has hitherto been its chief glory really set in in the Anglo-Saxon race? Has commercialism really throttled altruism? Has the era of the recognition of the inherent rights of men come to a close? Has our government lent its sanction to the code of international morals that accords the strong the right to rule the weak, brushing aside by the force of arms every claim of the weak? Alas! Alas!"

For many days Dorlan was very, very despondent. The *North* had voted to re-enthrone the Republican party without exacting of it a specific promise as to the regard to be had to the claims of the Filipinos to inherent equality. This amazed him. But as the political excitement subsided and he could feel the pulse of the American people apart from the influence of partizan zeal, he was the better able to analyze their verdict.

First, the failure to declare as to the ultimate status of the Filipinos was in a measure due to the politicians whose uniform policy is to postpone action on new problems until public sentiment has had time to crytallize. They were not quite certain as to what was the full import of the new national appetite and they were avoiding specific declarations until they could find out.

Secondly, the people of the North were in no mood to be hurried as to their policy with regard to the Filipinos. They had before them the example of Negroes of the South even then calling upon the North to return and set them free again. With this example of imperfect work before them the people of the North refused to be wrought up into a great frenzy of excitement over giving titular independence to the Filipinos.

Thirdly, Dorlan discovered that the election, instead of revealing a decline in altruism, on the contrary, gave evidence of the broadening and deepening of that spirit. He now saw in the verdict of the North the high resolve to begin at the very foundation and actually lift the Filipinos to such a plane that they would not only have freedom, but the power to properly exercise and preserve the same. Instead of losing its position as the teacher of nations, our government was, he saw, to confirm its title to that proud position. So nobly, so thoroughly, was it to do its work of leading the Filipinos into all the blessings of higher civilization, that other nations in contact with weaker peoples might find here a guide for their statesmen to follow. Thus he found written in the *hearts* of the noble people of the North the plank which provided adequately for the ultimate status of the Filipinos, which plank he had earnestly longed to see appear in the platforms of all political parties aspiring for the control of the government.

His faith in the people did not, however, influence him to forget that "eternal vigilance is the price of liberty." He was still of the opinion that the nation needed a balance wheel, needed a free lance ready to bear down upon all who, drunk with the wine of prosperity or maddened by greed for gain, might seek to lure the American people from the faith of the fathers.

Thus Dorlan, intending to begin anew his movement which we saw so tragically interrupted, returned to R——, only to suffer a second interruption in a manner now to be detailed.

One afternoon as Dorlan sat in his room in the city of R——, musing on the task before him, his elbows on the table and his noble, handsome face resting in his hands, rich music, as on a former oc-

casion more than a year ago, came floating up to
him. The music revealed the touch and the voice
of Morlene. He had not seen nor heard from her
since that eventful night on which she labored so
valiantly to save his life.

Dorlan arose and went down stairs with a view
to renewing his acquaintance with Morlene. He
knew nothing whatever of Harry's death, which
had transpired in his absence. Dorlan entered the
room where Morlene was playing. She turned to
receive the new comer whoever it might be. A
joyful exclamation escaped her lips when she per-
cieved that it was Dorlan.

"Mr. Warthell, I am so very glad to see you
alive and well. How often have I subjected my
actions to the closest scrutiny, disposed to accuse
myself of not doing all that might have been done
to prevent that dastardly assault upon you."

Dorlan was so entranced with Morlene's loveliness that he did not catch the full purport of
what she was saying. Morlene was clad in mourning and Dorlan was drinking in the beauty of her
loveliness in this new combination.

When Morlene finished her sentence and it was
incumbent upon Dorlan to reply, he was momenta-
rily embarrassed, not knowing what to say, having
lost what Morlene was saying by absorption in con-
templating her great beauty. It was tolerably
clear to him that her remark was one of solicitous

interest in himself, and after a very brief pause he said :

"Excuse me for not desiring to give attention to myself, in view of the fact that I am but now made aware by your mourning that some dear one has passed away."

"You have not heard, then," said Morlene, a look of sadness creeping over her face. She sat down on the piano stool whence she had arisen. "I have lost my husband. He was killed in the act of stopping some runaway horses more than a year ago."

Immediately there burst upon Dorlan's consciousness the thought that Morlene was free and that he might aspire for her hand. So great a hope thrust upon him so suddenly bewildered him by its very glory. Ordinarily imperturbable, even in the face of unexpected situations, he was now visibly agitated. He knew that he ought to frame words of condolence, but the new hope, springing from the secret chambers of his heart where he had long kept it in absolute bondage, clamored so loudly for a hearing that he could not deploy enough of his wits to speak in keeping with the amenities of the situation.

"Excuse me for a few moments, Mrs. Dalton," asked Dorlan, leaving the room. He went up the stairs leading to his room, taking two steps at a bound. Entering, he locked his door. Thrusting his hands into his pockets, he gazed abstractedly at the floor for a moment, then up at the ceiling. The word which as a boy he had used to denote great astonishment now came unbidden to his lips.

"Gee-whillikens!" he exclaimed. "And that divine woman is free! Thought, I wish you would sink into my consciousness at once," said Dorlan, apostrophizing. A few moments succeeded in imparting to him an outward look of calm. He then returned and expressed his feelings of condolence in words that suggested themselves to him as being appropriate. He soon excused himself from Morlene's presence with a view to rearranging his whole system of thinking so as to be in keeping with the new conditions with which he was thus unexpectedly confronted. "I have a little problem of desired expansion on my own hands, and I fear the government will have to wag along without me the best way it can for a while," said Dorlan to himself.

The ultimate status of Morlene Dalton was now of more importance to him than the ultimate status of the Filipinos.

CHAPTER XXIII.

A STREET PARADE.

A band of Negro musicians playing a popular air, was passing through the street on which Dorlan resided. He was in the act of going out of the gate as the procession got opposite to him, and paused to allow it to pass. There was a great concourse of Negro boys and girls, men and women, following the band of musicians. Their clothes were unclean, ragged and ill-fitting. Their faces and hands were soiled and seemed not to have been washed for many a day. The motley throng seemed to be utterly oblivious of its gruesome appearance, and all were walking along in boldness and with good cheer.

"Now those Negroes are moulding sentiment against the entire race," thought Dorlan, as his eye scanned the unsightly mass. "Be the requirement just or unjust the polished Negro is told to return and bring his people with him, before coming into possession of that to which his attainments would seem to entitle him. It is my opinion that there must be developed within the race a stronger altruistic tie before it can push forward at a proper gait. The classes must love the masses, in spite of the bad name the race is given by the indolent, the sloven and the criminal element." Taking another survey of the throng he said, "Ah! the squalor and misery of my poor voiceless race! What we see here is but a bird's-eye view. The heart grows sick when it contemplates the plight of the Negroes of the cities."

Dorlan's eye now wandered from the people to the band. In the midst of the musicians he saw a cart pulled by five dogs hitched abreast. In the cart stood a man holding aloft a banner which bore a peculiar inscription.

Dorlan read the inscription on the banner and looked puzzled. Coming out of his gate he kept pace with the procession, never withdrawing his eye from the banner. He read it the second, third, fourth and fifth times. At length he called out, "Hold! here am I." The occupant of the cart leapt up and gazed wildly over the throng, endeavoring to see the person that had spoken.

"Here," said Dorlan. The man looked at Dorlan, jumped from his cart and rushed through the crowd and ran to Dorlan's side. Taking a knife from his pocket he quickly made a slit in Dorlan's clothes just over the muscular part of his left arm. The purposes of the man were so evidently amicable that Dorlan interposed no objection. The man seemed to be satisfied with what he saw. He now threw himself at Dorlan's feet and uttered

loud exclamations of joy.   Arising he turned to
pay and dismiss the band.

The throng by this time was thoroughly excited
over the curious antics of the stranger, and had
clustered around Dorlan wondering what it was
that had caused such an abrupt cessation of the
open air concert which they were enjoying.   The
stranger now locked his arm in that of Dorlan and
the two returned to Dorlan's home.   The crowd
followed and stood for a long time at Dorlan's gate
hoping that the two would return and afford an
explanation.   As this did not happen, they at
length dispersed.

When Dorlan and the stranger entered the former's room and were seated, they looked at each
other in silence, Dorlan awaiting to be addressed
and the stranger seeking to further assure himself
that he was not mistaken.   He arose and again
looked at the markings on Dorlan's arm.   He now
spoke some words in a strange tongue.   Dorlan
readily replied in the same language.

The stranger now felt safe in beginning his
narrative.   Said he, in English, "My name is
Ulbah Kumi.   I hail from Africa.   I am one of an
army of commissioners sent out by our kingdom
into all parts of the world where Negroes have
been held in modern times as slaves.   We are hunt-
ing for the descendants of a lost prince.   This prince
was the oldest son of our reigning king, and was

taken captive in a battle fought with a rival kingdom. He was sold into slavery. The royal family
had a motto and a family mark. You recognized
the motto on the banner ; you have the royal mark.
You also look to be a prince. Tell me your family
history and I will make to you further disclosures."

Dorlan now told of his father and his grandfather. His grandfather had always claimed to be
the heir to an African throne, had imbued his, Dorlan's father, with that thought. The father had
taught the same to Dorlan. A certain formula,
said to be known to no others on earth, was cherished in their family.

"Now! Now!" said Kumi when Dorlan recited
that fact. "That formula is no doubt a key that
will unfold the hiding place of treasures that will
make you the richest man in the world. Here is
an inventory of what is to be found in that hiding
place."

Dorlan took the reputed inventory. The enormous value of the items cited staggered his imagination. ''This is incredulous,'' said Dorlan. "How
could Africans, unlearned in the values of civilized
nations, know how to store away these things."

"Easily explained," said Kumi. "A white explorer spent years in our kingdom collecting these
things. We deemed them worthless, gave them to
him readily and called him fool. He took sick in
our country and saw that he was going to die. He

called your great grandfather, our king, to his bedside, told him that civilization would make its way
into Africa one day, and urged him at all hazards
to preserve and secrete the treasures that he had
collected. Our king was led to believe that these
treasures would make him one of the greatest rulers
of earth, and he obeyed the dying man's injunc-
tion. The white man left this inventory and a
document giving the location of his European home,
the names and family history of his kin, asking
that our king remember them in the day of his
affluence.

"Our king gave the formula that leads to the
hiding place to your grandfather, your grandfather
told it to your father, your father has, I see, no
doubt, told it to you.

"As a further proof that I speak the truth I hand
you now a few specimen stones that were reserved
to prevent this affair from being classed as a myth."
He now took from a pocket a box of costly stones
and handed them to Dorlan.

"How these things would grace Morlene,"
thought Dorlan, as his eye passed from one spark-
ling jewel to another.

It now occurred to Dorlan that the acceptance of
this fortune might entail upon him a sacrifice of
which he was incapable. It might involve his leaving this country, a step that he could not even contemplate in view of the fact that Morlene was now
free. The looming of this contingency before his

mind caused him to drop the jewels as though they had suddenly become hot. Kumi looked up at him in great astonishment.

Dorlan's face now wore a pained expression. He had always been profoundly interested in Africa and was congratulating himself on the opportunity now offered to convert the proffered kingdom into an enlightened republic. It now seemed that his own interests and those of his ancestral home were about to clash. He cannot endure the thought of putting an ocean between Morlene and himself. Nor can he with equanimity think of allowing Africa to remain in her existing condition.

"When am I expected to go to Africa?" enquired Dorlan in serious tones.

"You may not have to come at all, and yet serve our purpose."

"How so?" asked Dorlan, arising and drawing near to Kumi.

The latter began: "We Africans are engaged in a sociological investigation of many questions. We are seeking to know definitely what part the climate, the surface, the flora and the fauna have played in keeping us in civilization's back yard. Huxley thinks that our woolly hair and black skins came to us only after our race took up its abode in Africa. He holds that it was nature's contribution to render us immune from the yellow fever germs so abundant in swampy regions.

"He thinks that those of our race who did not take on a dark hue and woolly texture of hair were the less adapted to life in the tropics and eventually died out, leaving those that were better adjusted to survive.

"He thinks that these beneficial modifications were preserved and transmitted with increasing strength from generation to generation until our hue and our hair or the physical attributes for which they stand rendered us immune from yellow fever. I may add that Livingstone says of us, 'Heat alone does not produce blackness of skin, but heat with moisture seems to insure the deepest hue.'

"Now, nature, in thus protecting us against yellow fever, by changing our color from the original, whatever it was, has painted upon us a sign that causes some races to think that there is a greater difference between us and them than there really is. So much for our color and the ills that it has entailed."

Dorlan interrupted Kumi to remark very feelingly:

"I am truly glad that you are not inoculated with that utterly nonsensical view to be met with in this country, which represents that the Negro's color is the result of a curse pronounced by Noah upon his recovery from a drunken stupor. Please proceed."

Kumi resumed his remarks. " Mr. Herbert Spencer holds that our comparative lack of energy is due to heat and *moisture*. He states that 'the earliest recorded civilizatibn grew up in a hot and dry region—Egypt; and in hot and dry regions also arose the Babylonian, Assyrian and Phœnician civilizations.' He points out that all 'the conquering races of the world have hailed from within or from the borders of the hot and dry region marked on the rain map ' rainless districts,' and extending across North Africa, Arabia, Persia, and on through Thibet into Mongolia.'

" He, therefore, would ascribe our backwardness principally to a woful lack of energy, a condition brought on by our hot and moist climate.

"When our investigation of these questions is complete," continued Kumi, " we will know just what has brought us where we are and can determine whether artificial appliances sufficient to counteract existing influences can be discovered and instituted.

" Mr. Benjamin Kidd seems to think that the tropics can never develop the highest type of civilization. In the event that the government of the tropics is to be conducted from the temperate zones, we tropical people will desire Negroes to remain in the temperate zones, to advocate such policies and form such alliances as shall be for our highest good.

" So, it may turn out to be the best for you, our king, to remain here, for our welfare, owing to our peculiar environments, depends, just now, as much upon what others think of us as upon what we ourselves may do. The question of your going to Africa is not, therefore, a pressing one, yet."

"That leaves me somewhat free to deal with a question that *is* pressing, and pressing hard," said Dorlan, clasping Kumi's hand in joy, now that the way was clear for him to serve without conflict his own heart and the home of his fathers.

Kumi looked at Dorlan puzzled as to what question it was that was pressing for a settlement. Dorlan did not enlighten him on the subject, however.

But we know, do we not, dear reader?

CHAPTER XXIV.

GOING FORTH TO UNFETTER.

Morlene was yet wearing mourning for Harry, and, as a consequence, Dorlan was forced to delay the inauguration of his suit. If you think that this procedure, or rather non-procedure, was to his liking, but ask the stars unto whom his heart so often entrusted its secrets; ask the wee small hours of the night who saw him restless, times without number.

Somehow his business seemed to require him to pass Morlene's house rather often; and yet the business could not have been so very urgent, in that he found so much time to spare, talking to Morlene in an informal way at her gate. And, to go further, if the truth must out, Morlene's presence at that gate at Dorlan's time of passing did happen, we must admit, rather often to be placed in the category with usual *accidental* occurrences.

Now and then, at rare intervals, Dorlan would pay Morlene a call on some matter of business, he would say. On those occasions it was interesting to note how quickly the business matter was disposed of—in fact, was so often actually forgotten by Dorlan and, it must be confessed, by Morlene, too.

The truth of the matter is, to be plain, these two

individuals had discovered that their souls were congenial spirits, each seeming to need the other, if it
would have a sense of completeness. Now, this
was the latent Dorlan and the latent Morlene, the
apparent Dorlan and the apparent Morlene co-operating with society in its policy of adding to the
duration of the marriage vow, which reads until
death, but which has been stretched by society to
an indefinite period thereafter. This discovery of a
bond of affinity, we say, was purely the work of the
latent Dorlan and the latent Morlene, for were not
those two members of society abstaining from all
mention of the regard, the deep regard, the boundless—— excuse us, the period of mourning has not
passed.

One day Dorlan discovered by consulting his
memorandum that about the usual time between
those business (?) propositions had elapsed and he
searched his mind for a plausible excuse for making
a call.

When Dorlan arrived at Morlene's home that
night, imagine his feelings when he saw on entering the parlor that she had at last laid aside her
mourning attire. The thought that she was now
approachable set his soul ablaze.

What Dorlan took to be the most wicked of all
demons, seemed to say to him, "Don't declare yourself on this the very first occasion. Those gate
talks and business visits are not supposed to have
been acts of courtship, remember."

"Will you please leave me?" whispered Dorlan's soul to the imaginary grinning demon that made the suggestion.

Utterly repudiating all thought of further delay, Dorlan drew close to Morlene. She saw the love signals in Dorlan's eyes. Rather than have her soul flash back replies, she inclined her head forward and looking down, clutched the table near which she stood.

"Morlene," said Dorlan, "I really believe that my heart will burst if I do not let out its secret. Morlene, I love you. But you know that and you know how well. You have read this and more, too, in my countenance. Will you be my wife?"

Those words spoken into Morlene's ear at close range were elixir unto her soul. Looking up into Dorlan's face, her eyes told of love, deep, boundless. This Dorlan saw. But he saw more than love. He saw despair written so legibly upon that sweet face that it could not be misunderstood and would not be ignored.

"Come," said Dorlan, leading Morlene to a seat. Sitting down by her side and taking one of her lovely hands in his, he said in tones charged with deepest emotion :

"Tell me, dear girl, that you will be my wife. May I, poor worm of the dust, be allowed to call you my own?" plead Dorlan, bestowing on Morlene that peculiar look born of love stirred to its depths by anxiety.

"I do not know, Mr. Warthell, I do not know. It ——"

"Do not know," gasped Dorlan, dropping the hand tenderly. "My God! she does not know!" he groaned.

"Wait but a second, and all will be plain," said Morlene, placing a hand upon Dorlan's arm and looking eagerly into his grief-torn face.

"Wait a second," repeated Dorlan mechanically. "A second in moments like these seems akin to an eternity. But I wait."

"Now, Mr. Warthell, be fair to yourself," said Morlene, soothingly. "You remarked that I must have read some things in your countenance. Remember your soul has an eyesight, and you have done some reading, too." Her eyes were averted, her tones low, her speech halting as she made this half-confession to Dorlan's eager ears.

Dorlan, who had been feeling more like an arctic explorer than a suitor for a lady's hand, felt his blood running warmer from the effects of this morsel of cheer.

"I will explain to you what it is that I do not know, Mr. Warthell. I do not know how long it will be before conditions in the South will warrant women of my way of thinking in becoming wives of men of your mould."

"If," said Dorlan, rising, "consideration of this matter is to be postponed until my environments enable me to prove myself worthy of you, my doom is certain. For the most benign influences of earth have not produced the man that could claim your hand on the ground of merit."

"Mr. Warthell, you misapprehend. A second thought would have told you not to place a construction on my remarks that causes them to savor of egotism on my part. It is far from me to suggest that anything is needed to make you worthy of any woman. To the contrary, your esteem is a tribute than which there is nothing higher, so I feel. Now, hear me calmly," said Morlene.

"Not until I have purged myself of contempt," said Dorlan, deferentially.

"I hold that egotism is inordinate self-esteem, esteem carried beyond what is deserved. Under this definition, show me, please, how you could manifest egotism. It is absolutely unthinkable from my point of view."

Morlene waved her hand deprecatingly, told Dorlan to be seated and began an explanation of the peculiar situation in which they found themselves. Dorlan was calmer now; he realized an undercurrent of love in all that Morlene was saying and he knew, as all men know, that love will eventually assert itself. So he bore Morlene's attempt to tie cords about her affections, much in the spirit of one who might see a web woven across the sky for the feet of the sun.

Morlene said : " Mr. Warthell, to my mind it is the function of the wife to idealize the aims of a husband, to quicken the energies that would flag, to be at once the incentive and perennial inspiration of his noble achievements, to point him to the stars and steady his hand as he carves his name upon the skies. In the South the Negro wife is robbed of this holy task. We are being taught in certain high quarters that self-repression is the Negro's chiefest virtue. Our bodies are free— they no longer wear the chains, but our spirits are yet in fetters. I have firmly resolved, Mr. Warthell, to accept no place by a husband's side until I can say to his spirit, "Go forth to fill the earth with goodness and glory."

Morlene paused for an instant.

" Mr. Warthell, in you may slumber the genius of a Pericles, but a wife in the South dare not urge upon you to become a town constable or a justice of the peace. Talk about slavery ! Ah ! the chains that fetter the body are but as ropes of down when compared to those that fetter the mind, the spirit of man. And think ye I would enter your home simply to inspire that great soul of yours to restlessness and fruitless tuggings at its chains ! In the day when a Negro has a man's chance in the race of life, I will let my heart say to you, Mr. Warthell, all that it wishes to say."

Morlene ceased speaking and the two sat long in silence. Dorlan was the first to speak,

"Morlene, I confess I am a slave. My neighbors, my white fellow citizens, have formed a pen, have drawn a zigzag line about me and told me that I must not step across on pain of death. Having a mind as other men, such arbitrary restrictions are galling. I am then a slave, limited not by my capacity to feel and do, but by the color of my skin. You do not wish to marry a slave; refuse him for his own good. All of that is clear to me, and I chide you not. Come! There are lands where a man's color places no restrictions on his aspirations for what is high and useful. Let us flee thither!"

"No, no, no, Mr. Warthell! Let us not flee. At least, not yet. Our dignity as a people demands that the manhood rights of the race be recognized on every foot of soil on which the sun sees fit to cast his rays."

"Now, Morlene," said Dorlan, "you as good as tell me that you will never be my wife. Pray, tell me, why am I so rudely tossed about upon the bosom of life's heaving ocean?" These words were spoken in tones of utter despair.

"I have not said that I would not be your wife, Dorlan. I am trying every day I live to devise a solution for our Southern problem."

"She called me Dorlan, she called me Dorlan," said he to himself, rejoicing inwardly over this fresh burst of sunshine just as his gloom was deepening. Suddenly his face showed the illumination of a great hope.

"Morlene! Morlene!" cried Dorlan, in a rush of enthusiasm, "Suppose I, Dorlan Warthell, solve this problem; suppose I unfetter the mind of the Negro and allow it full scope for operation; suppose I offer to you a thoroughly substantial hope of racial regeneration, will you——" Here Dorlan paused and looked lovingly into the sweet face upturned to his. "If I do these things," he resumed in sober tone, "will you be my wife?"

"Mr. Warthell, if you can open the way for me to really be your wife, there is nothing in my heart that bids me shrink from the love you offer."

Dorlan's mind entertained one great burst of hope, then fled at once to the great race problem that had hung pall-like over the heads of the American people for so many generations, and now stood between himself and Morlene. A sense of the enormity of the task that he had undertaken now overwhelmed him. Dorlan bowed his head, the following thoughts coursing through his agitated mind: "I am to weld two heterogeneous elements into a homogeneous entity. I am to make a successful blend of two races that differ so widely as do the whites and the Negroes. Each race has manifested its racial instincts, and has shown us all, that wise planning must take account of these. The problem is inherently a difficult one and of a highly complex nature. But with an incentive such as I have, surely it can be solved,

Thomas Jefferson and Abraham Lincoln said the problem was incapable of solution, that the two races could not live together on terms of equality. They were great and wise, but not infallible. With Morlene as a prize, I shall prove them wrong." Morlene, taking advantage of his abstraction, bestowed on him an unreserved look of pitying love.

Dorlan looked up suddenly from his reverie, and their eyes met once more. There was no reserve now and Dorlan's joy was so keen that it seemed to pain him. Arising to go, he said : " I go from you consecrating my whole power to the task before me. Fortunate it is, indeed, for the South that she has at least one man so surrounded that he cannot be happy himself until he makes this wilderness of woe blossom as a rose. Farewell."

Dorlan now left and walked slowly toward his home. He reflected, " I will have no business at her home now until this problem is solved. Suppose I do not solve it."

Dorlan's fears began to assert themselves. " I may never, never see that face again. Think of it !" he said. This thought was too much for Dorlan. He paused, leaned upon the fence, thrust his hat back from his fevered brow. He turned and retraced his steps to Morlene's home. She met him at the door and was not surprised at his return. Her heart was craving for just another sight of its exiled lord. Re-entering the parlor, they stood facing each other.

"Morlene," said Dorlan, "I have come to ask a boon of you. I can labor so much better with a full assurance of your love. From your eyes, from your words, I say humbly, I have come to feel that you have honored me with that love. But the testimony is incomplete. Will you grant unto me the one remaining assurance? Will you seal our most holy compact with a kiss?"

Morlene's lips parted not, but she attempted an answer, nevertheless. Her queenlike head was shaking negatively, saying, "Please do not require that." But those telltale eyes were saying, "Why, young man the whole matter rests with you." Morlene was conscious that her eyes were contradicting the negative answer that her head was giving. To punish the two beautiful traitors she turned them away from Dorlan and made them look at the carpet. Morlene in this attitude was so exquisitely beautiful that Dorlan was powerless to resist the impulse that made him take her into his arms.

One rapturous kiss, and Dorlan was gone!

CHAPTER XXV.

TONY MARSHALL.

Tony Marshall was one of the Negroes of the younger class who had left the country district and had come to R—— as a result of the imbroglio between Lemuel Dalton and Harry Dalton. He had come to the city with the untried innocence of country life, sober, industrious and frugal, acceptable as a wholesome infusion into Negro life in the city, which, so far as the masses were concerned, stood sadly in need thereof. Without much difficulty he had secured work as a porter in a hardware store. After a few years' sojourn in the city, he had fallen in love and married.

Among the Negroes of R—— Mrs. Tony Marshall was variously designated as "a good looking woman," "a fine looking woman," and among the older ones as "a likely gal;" and she richly deserved these encomiums passed on her personal appearance. She was not a small woman, nor yet could you call her large. Her form, while not delicately chiseled, presented an appearance that seemed to be a satisfactory compromise between beauty and strength, each struggling to be noted in this one form. Her face was well featured, her hazle colored eyes making it very attractive. As to com-

plexion, she was dark, quite dark, and of a hue so
soft and attractive therewith that her complexion
made her an object of envy.

Tony Marshall adored his wife, and it was his
one ambition to see her happy. Everything that
he did was with a view to her comfort and happiness. On the meagre wages which he received he
had not been able to provide for her as he had desired.

Noticing that young white men who had entered
the employ of the hardware company after his coming and knew no more of the requirements of the
business than he did—noticing that these had several times been promoted, Tony Marshall made an
application for an increase in his wages. The head
of the firm looked at him in astonishment. It was
an unwritten and inexorable rule in that and in
many other establishments that the wages of Negro
employes were to remain the same forever, however
efficient the labor and however long the term of
service.

Failing of promotion where he was, and noting
that the rate of one dollar per day prevailed almost universally, Tony Marshall saw no relief in
changing employment, and decided to increase his
own wages at his employers' expense. He made a
comparison between the salary which he was receiving and that being received by the white em-
ployees who did work similar in character to his. He
began, therefore, to purloin the wares of the com-

pany and dispose of them at various pawn shops. As a "sop" to his conscience he stole only so much as sufficed to bring his wages to the level of others who did work like his. His thefts were the more easily committed because he had won the unlimited confidence of his employers.

Tony has just rented a more commodious house for the pleasure of his wife, and as his rent is to be increased, he is pondering how to further increase his income. On this particular morning when our story finds him, he is debating this question as he walks to his work. At last he concluded to steal that day a very fine pistol from the stock under his care, which theft he hoped would net him such a nice sum that he could suspend pilfering for a while. When he returned home that evening he carried the pistol with him, and hid it under the front door-step, it being his rule to not allow his wife to know anything of his misdoings; for he could not bear the thought of forfeiting her respect.

"I am going to my lodge meeting now; I may not return until very late," said Tony that night, as he kissed his wife good-bye. Instead of going to the lodge meeting, however, Tony Marshall went to the section of the city where were congregated practically all of the vicious Negroes of R——. Entering a house, the front room of which was the abode of an aged couple, he passed to the rear through a hall way. Giving the proper rap at a door, he was admitted. He was now in a long room well crowded with Negro men and many women, who sat at tables engaged in various kinds of gaming.

The occupants of the room gazed up at the newcomer, quickly, enquiringly, but seeing that it was the well known Tony, their attention returned to the matters before them. The flapping of cards, the rolling of dice, outbursts of profanity, the clinking of glasses as liquor drinking progressed, were the sounds that filled the room.

Tony found room at a dice table and was soon deeply engaged in the game. At a late hour the accustomed rap was heard at the door and it was opened. Great was the consternation of all when the newcomers were discovered to be a half dozen policemen.

The inmates of the gambling house saw at once that some frequenter of the place had proven traitor and furnished the officers with information. They were all placed under arrest and formed into a line to be marched to the city jail. The Negroes had submitted with such good grace that the officers felt able to dispense with the patrol wagon, the jail being near.

Tony Marshall's thoughts were of his wife, Lula. She was of a highly respectable family and her mortification would be boundless should she know of his arrest in the gambling den and hear of his being in the chain gang working out his fine on the public highways.

Tony Marshall decided to escape at the risk of his life. The gambling fraternity had a code of signals that could give the cue to the proper course to be pursued under any given circumstances. The leader of the gang now gave three coughs, which meant, "Raise a row among yourselves." The idea was to get up a fight among the prisoners and while the officers were attempting to quell the fight, as many as could were to make their escape. It was the rule that all who made their escape were to employ lawyers and raise money to help out those left behind.

A group began quarreling among themselves, and a fight soon followed. The officers interposed to quell the disturbance and prisoners broke and ran in all directions. The officers found that they had a larger number than they could well manage under the circumstances, and they gave their attention to corralling a few, letting the others escape in the hope of tracing them out and re-arresting them on the morrow.

Among those that escaped was Tony Marshall. Running by his home, he secured the stolen pistol from beneath the doorstep, got his bicycle from the woodhouse and was soon speeding out of the city. He chose the road that led to the settlement whence he had come to the city. It was his intention from that point to write to his wife, telling her that he had received a most urgent call to see his aged mother who was represented to him to be dying.

Throughout the night Tony rode at a rapid rate, putting many miles between himself and the city. About daybreak, as he was speeding along on his bicycle, he glanced up into a tree and saw therein a squirrel. "Good luck!" said he, "there is my breakfast." Jumping from his bicycle, he got on the side of the road opposite to the tree that held the squirrel. Elevating his pistol, he took aim and was upon the eve of pulling the trigger when he heard the clatter of the hoofs of a horse galloping in his direction. He dropped the pistol to his side and peered around the bend of the road to catch sight of the newcomer on the scene. For a few minutes only we leave him standing thus that we may fully acquaint you with the newcomer, that the horror of the meeting between the two may not come as too great a shock to you.

"But how is the waiting, struggling, hoping Dorlan concerned in all of this?" the reader asks. That, too, in due time will be apparent.

CHAPTER XXVI.

A MORNING RIDE.

We are at the Dalton house once more. It is the night on which we followed Tony Marshall to the gambling den, which we saw raided by the officers of the law. Under the window of Lemuel Dalton's bed room a dog had stationed himself, and throughout the night uttered long, loud and piteous howls.

Lemuel Dalton professed to be above superstition and detested that in the Negroes more than he did anything else, perhaps. While professing to the contrary, he was in reality superstitious to a marked degree, even against his own better sense. This semi-consciousness of the presence of a latent superstition in the crevices of his inner-self, no doubt served to intensify his antipathies against a people who had thus in spite of himself injected superstition into him; for he blamed the Negroes for the prevalence of superstition in the Southern States. So the howling of this homeless dog bothered Lemuel, although he sought to assure himself, over and over again, that it did not. He had arisen more than once and fired his pistol out of the window in order to stop the noise of the dog. The dog would quiet down for a brief period and then resume his canine lamentations. The howling of the dog, coupled with its persistence, produced in Lemuel Dalton a state of mind bordering on terror. The Negroes held that the howling of a dog be-neath a window was a sure sign that an inmate of the house was soon to die.

Arising very early the next morning, Lemuel Dalton entered his library and took a seat. He wheeled his chair until it faced the east window and, tilting back in it, mechanically twirled his mustache, a look of deep meditation coming over his face. " Confound the people who first brought the Negroes to this country," he said. He was worried that he could not shake off the superstition as to death following the howling of a dog.

In the midst of his broodings Lemuel Dalton's pretty little wife (for he is married now) came dash-ing into the room attired in a riding habit. Lem-uel Dalton wheeled around to meet her and her quick eye caught the cloud that was just vanishing from his face.

" Lemuel, my dear, what on earth are you allow-ing to trouble you?" she said, shaking her riding whip at him, playfully, while her eyes were shining with the love that she cherished for him.

" I may tell you when you return from your morning ride," he said, opening his arms to receive his wife.

" You naughty lad," she cried, looking into his eyes with mock earnestness. "When did you ever hear of a woman consenting to wait a moment to obtain a secret? Tell me *now* on pain of being doomed to bear this burden, my humble self, in your arms for ever."

"The very penalty that you affix as a menace is an inducement for me to disobey. I resist the temptation, however, and tell you the subject of my thoughts. I was thinking of the Negroes."

A shiver ran over the frame of Mrs. Dalton and the cheerful smile died out of her face. "Lemuel, will you people of the South ever be rid of this eternal nightmare?" queried Mrs. Dalton, looking up into Lemuel's face.

Lemuel tenderly stroked her beautiful hair, but did not essay to answer her question. The fact of the matter was, he regarded the Negro problem as growing graver and more complicated as time wore on. The strenuous efforts of the Negro to rise and the decrease of the distance between the two races he viewed with alarm. He did not care to communicate his real feelings to his wife, so he said nothing.

Mrs. Dalton's nature was of a light and volatile kind and she thought of the Negroes only for an instant. Wresting herself out of her husband's arms, she skipped out of the room. She immediately reappeared at the door of the library and threw a kiss at Lemuel in girlish fashion and was soon mounted and riding out to get the benefit of the brisk morning air. As she saunters along, we may learn a few points in her history that bear upon the case unto which events are leading. She was born and reared in a section of the State of Maine where no Negroes whatever live. It was here that Lemuel Dalton found, wooed, and wedded her. She had read from time to time of the crimes of brutal Negroes and the summary punishments administered to them, and she had rather imperceptibly grown to regard the prevailing race type of the Negroes as being criminal. This opinion was not an unnatural outgrowth of the newspaper habit of giving unlimited space and flaming headlines to the vicious Negro, the exotic, while the many millions who day by day went uncomplainingly to their daily tasks and wrought worthily for the country's welfare, received but scant attention.

The opinion that this state of affairs caused Mrs. Dalton to imbibe, was the further fostered by the atmosphere of the Dalton house, which was so thoroughly hostile to the Negro. The whole of the Dalton place was now manned by white help, and Negroes would not so much as go there on errands of business. It was from such a home and under the conditions outlined that Mrs. Dalton went forth for her morning ride.

It was the noise of Mrs. Dalton's horse that caused Tony Marshall to pause in his attempt to kill the squirrel.

CHAPTER XXVII.

THEY FEAR EACH OTHER.

As Tony peered around the bend in the road, Mrs. Dalton caught sight of him and uttered a piercing scream. Tony knew the horse to be that of Lemuel Dalton and he perceived at once that the situation was full of danger for him, as the unintentional frightening of white women in the South had furnished more than one victim for the mob. Knowing so well the feelings of Lemuel Dalton toward Negroes, he reasoned that if the white woman who had become frightened at him, returned to the house and reported that she had come upon a Negro with a drawn pistol, public opinion among the whites would at once adjudge him guilty of harboring a purpose of committing a dastardly crime against woman's honor. He knew that a strong suspicion to this effect meant instant and violent death to the party suspected. He was determined to see to it that the woman did not leave him in a disturbed frame of mind. Rushing forward, he grasped the horse's bridle. This all the more frightened and excited Mrs. Dalton.

"Lady," said Tony, fear in every lineament of

his face;"Lady," he repeated, in anxious tones, "don't be afraid. I am not going to harm you."

Mrs. Dalton instinctively looked down at the pistol, which seemed to be a contradiction to his words.

Seeing the look and interpreting it, Tony said, "There, I have thrown it away," accompanying his words with the casting of the pistol by the roadside.

Mrs. Dalton yet said nothing, her eye following the pistol. She noted that Tony had not thrown it very far away.

Tony, who was studying her countenance with a full knowledge of the fact that his life depended upon the outcome of the interview, read her impression that the casting aside of the pistol was but a ruse. "Lady," said Tony, " I have caught hold of your horse to keep you from going away from me frightened, for the white people will kill me on a mere suspicion of wrong intention on my part. I am harmless. I used to live out here."

This last remark increased Mrs. Dalton's agitation. She had heard of Harry Dalton, knew nothing of his death and feared that this was he, returning for vengeance.

" I got into trouble in the city and am running away. That's how I am out here so early."

"Oh, he is a criminal," said Mrs. Dalton, excitedly."

Tony saw that talking did not better his case, so he stopped. He bowed his head to meditate.

Mrs. Dalton thought that he was planning an attack, and her agitation was increasing every second.

"Plague on it!" said Tony. "I am in a pretty fix. I'll swear I wish those 'cops' had me safe in prison. I have swapped the witch for the devil."

Addressing Mrs. Dalton he said: "Well, lady, I'll let you go and take my chances."

As soon as Tony turned loose the bridle Mrs. Dalton gave whip to her horse, intending to flee as fast as the speed of the animal would permit. Tony saw that his action in turning the horse loose had not inspired confidence in the woman and that she was leaving him fully impressed that his purposes were evil. He now decided to take advantage of every circumstance that he could to save his life.

Seizing his pistol, he ran forward and fired, intending to kill the horse and thus have a better chance to escape before the woman could reach her home and start others in pursuit. At his second shot the horse reared and Mrs. Dalton fell off to the ground. The horse also fell, a part of his huge frame falling upon and crushing her prostrate form.

When Tony Marshall saw what he had done, he turned to flee. Proceeding a short distance, he halted. "I must go back to find out whether the woman is dead," he said. He therefore turned and walked in a timorous manner toward the fallen woman. "Some one may have heard the shot and may be hurrying here," he thought, and halted again, casting furtive glances first up and then down the road. "What, oh, what have I done to be in such a fix!" he exclaimed in terror.

Continuing to look about him fearfully, Tony approached the spot where the horse and the woman lay. By dint of hard labor, he succeeded in removing that portion of the horse that lay upon her. He was overjoyed to find from her pulse that she was still alive. "What must I do next," he said. He sat down to meditate. "I haven't yet murdered anybody and I shall not let this woman die if I can help it," he said with determination.

Tony arose and, going to Mrs. Dalton, lifted her in his arms and proceeded in the direction of her home. After many pauses by the wayside for rest, he at last reached the Dalton estate. Through the window of his library, Lemuel Dalton saw his wife being brought home to him in an apparently lifeless condition. At once Morlene's prophecy came back to him. Raising the window and leaping out, he rushed to meet Tony and gathered his wife in his arms.

"Eulalie! Eulalie! Oh! Eulalie!" he cried. "Speak to me, beloved."

"Lemuel," she murmured, as she looked at him out of half opened eyes.

"Thank God! Oh! Thank God, she lives," he exclaimed, bearing his wife rapidly yet tenderly to her bedroom.

The family physician was summoned and he hastened to the bedside with all possible speed. Only a slight examination, however, was needed to disclose the fact that human skill would be of no avail.

CHAPTER XXVIII.

"O DEATH, WHERE IS THY STING?"

Dorlan had just drawn down the curtains to the windows of his room, thus bringing to a close the contest that the artificial light of the room was waging with the fading twilight, the last feeble protest of the sun, for that day deposed. He was standing before his desk which was strewn with books, pamphlets and newspaper clippings, bearing on the subject engaging his attention, when suddenly his door was thrust open.

Quickly turning to learn who his unceremonious visitor was, Dorlan saw the Hon. Hezekiah T. Bloodworth standing in the doorway pointing a pistol toward him. The pistol hand swayed to and fro, signifying the unsteadiness of a drunken man, while Bloodworth's bloated face and reddened eyes emphasized the fact of his debauchery.

"Oh—hic—yes—hic—I've got—hic-hic-hic you-hic. I'll—hic—kill—hic—hic—you—hic," stammered Bloodworth, attempting to impart force enough to his unsteady fingers to pull the trigger of the pistol.

Dorlan started in the direction of the drunken man intending to disarm him. Just then some one

(194)

implanted a blow upon the base of Bloodworth's skull, which sent that gentleman to the floor in a sprawling attitude. The pistol which was in Bloodworth's hand exploded upon striking the floor, but no serious damage resulted.

A tall, somewhat slender white man had delivered the blow. This stranger now forced Bloodworth to rise and accompany him down the stairs. Bloodworth whined after the manner of a child, as he staggered along. The stranger hailed a passing policeman and handed Bloodworth over to him. He then returned to Dorlan's room. As he entered, Dorlan was struck with the look of sorrow so legibly written in the face of the man. Such utter woe Dorlan had never before seen depicted in a human countenance. The man, though invited to sit down, declined to do so.

Looking Dorlan in the face, the stranger said, "My name is Lemuel Dalton. I perceive that you glean from my countenance that fate has hurled its harpoon into my soul." Lemuel Dalton's frame shook as a tempest of emotions swept through him. "My wife," he continued, " the most beautiful, the most angelic, the most beloved woman of earth, has been needlessly slain."

Dorlan was listening with absorbing interest and evident sympathy.

"Circumstances killed my wife, sir. Circumstances—cold, cruel, circumstances." Lemuel Dalton paused as though desiring to give his words ample opportunity to convey their awful message. "It was on this wise," he resumed. "She met a Negro who was fleeing from justice. She had heard so much of late of the crimes of Negroes against white women that she was terribly fright_ ened by the mere fact of seeing this Negro. The Negro was frightened over the consequences likely to ensue as a result of her fright. He sought to reassure her. She mistrusted him the more. To keep her from reaching me in time to institute a successful pursuit, the Negro killed the horse that she was riding. The horse in falling caught my wife partially under his huge frame. She was fatally injured."

Lemuel Dalton now turned away from Dorlan to hide the tears that had gathered in his eyes. "She died," said he, in broken tones. "On her dying bed she begged me to not prosecute the Negro on the charge of murder. In her last moments she said to me, 'Lemuel, good bye. Save other homes from a like fate. Dispel this atmosphere of suspicion in which I have been stifled unto my death.' I have obeyed her request with regard to the Negro. A careful investigation demonstrated that he had told my wife and me the truth in every detail. He is now in prison serving his sentence for the offenses committed prior to his chance meeting with my wife."

Pointing his finger at Dorlan he raised his tremulous voice and said in ringing tones, "Do you realize, sir, that the social fabric of which you are a part, furnished the viper that has stung me in a vital spot? Where, sir, are your churches, your school rooms, all of your influences that are supposed to produce worthy beings?" Lemuel Dalton's manner was so frantic that Dorlan began to feel that he was dangerously near insanity.

Lemuel Dalton divined the thought that was passing through Dorlan's mind and answered it, lowering his voice as he did so. "Oh, no! I am not at all unbalanced. To show you that I am not I shall answer my own question. You Negroes need more from us Southern whites than a feeling of indifference, or a spirit of 'make it if you can.' I have come to learn at so sad a cost that the safety and happiness of my race is inexorably bound up with the virtue and well-being of your race." The look of intensity now faded from his face; a sort of vacant expression appeared.

As though listlessly looking at something in the distance, he said, half musingly, "Morlene Dalton sent me to you. I went to her because she told me years ago that I would come to this. I am here to-night to offer my help to your race, and to ask what you all desire of me." He spoke slowly and in solemn tones.

"But, hold! before you speak, let me tell you

that about me which is subject to no compromise," he burst forth excitedly. Said he: "I am an exclusive; I want no mixture of blood, thought or activities with the Negro race. I want this white race to keep on manifesting its true inwardness to the world. I wish our whole civilization to be permeated with our own peculiar fragrance and that only. Whatever I can do for your people without jeopardy to this conception I stand ready to do. True, this means that I desire you to be an alien in our midst. But my present position is an improvement on my former, in that I am now willing to do all that can be done to make this alien, happy, prosperous and virtuous; but an alien ever, remember. Will you kindly point out to a white man standing on this platform what *he* may consistently do for the Negro?"

Lemuel Dalton ceased speaking and now sat in the chair which he had previously refused.

"I am grieved, profoundly grieved that your wife, who may be the prototype of hundreds, has been drawn into the awful vortex of this race trouble."

Lemuel Dalton arose from his seat and with glaring eyes looked down upon Dorlan intently.

Again the impression came to Dorlan that he was dealing with a mad man, and he began to ponder a line of action based on that thought.

"Tut, tut, you persist in thinking I am crazy,"

said Lemuel Dalton, again guessing Dorlan's thoughts and bringing his will to bear to cause a more calm expression to appear on his (Lemuel's) face.

Drawing near to Dorlan, he said : "I came to discuss the race question with you, but I am in no mood for that." He paused for an instant. Resuming in a lower tone of voice, he said, slowly, "You colored folks believe in God. I don't." Again he paused. "That is, I didn't. But the morning Eulalie, my wife, was brought home wounded, I called God's name for the first time since my early childhood." Here he paused again.

"Eulalie was a Christian," he said, looking into Dorlan's face piercingly. "Tell me the truth. Do you, do you," he asked falteringly. "Do you think that—" here a pause—"I shall meet—Eulalie again?" The last words were uttered in a loud screeching voice. Without waiting for an answer Lemuel Dalton turned away to hide his fast falling tears. Out of the room he walked, out into the darkness he went, alternately imploring and cursing the great force, whatever it might be, that was operating through all creation, and had suffered so terrible a load to fall upon his shoulders.

As for Dorlan, he sat far into the night musing on the occurrences of the evening. "To-night I have been confronted with an epitome of the situation of the Negro in this country," he said. "One white man comes who is angry because I will not be his tool. Then follows the exclusive, who feels that my touch is contaminating. Truly the Negro is between the upper and the nether millstones.

"Ah, Morlene what a task you have assigned unto this pilot, called by you to guide the bark of the Negro over this perilous sea. As I take my post, happy am I, that in my love of humanity I find my chart; in my love for my race I have a compass; and in my love for you I have a lighthouse on the shore.

"Shine on, sweet soul, that I may pilot this vessel through the breakers, above whose hidden heads the waves are ever chanting the solemn song of death."

Happy was Dorlan in this hour that his inherited riches would enable him to conquer ills which the poverty of the race had hitherto rendered insurmountable.

CHAPTER XXIX.

IN THE BALANCES.

At last the day came on which Dorlan was to submit his plan to Morlene.

He arose early that morning, packed his trunk, boxed up his most important papers and wrote out instructions as to the disposition to be made of his other possessions. These preparations completed, he walked down town to the post office and sent his plan to Morlene as registered matter. Having done this, Dorlan returned to his boarding place and bade all a sorrowful good-bye, stating that a great deal of uncertainty was attendant upon his journey, and that he knew not whether he would ever return to R——. Going down to the depot, he was soon aboard a train speeding away.

In the meanwhile Morlene had received the documents sent to her. In addition to the plan, Dorlan had sent a personal letter, on the envelope of which were written these words, "Please do not read the enclosed letter until you have read and passed upon the plan." Morlene lifted the envelope to her lips, kissed it, and laid it away, intend-

ing to read the letter after her study of the plan,
in keeping with Dorlan's wishes.

Morlene was deeply conscious as to how much
depended upon her verdict on Dorlan's plan.   Her
own and the happiness of Dorlan were involved.
The suffering, restless Negroes were to be offered a panacea and she was their representative to
accept or reject the proffered medicine.   The welfare of the South and the peace of the nation were at
stake.   Upon the outcome of the race question in
America the hopes of the darker races of the world
depended.   Even the cause of popular government
was involved, she felt, for it was to be seen whether
a republic could deal with a race problem of so
virulent a type.   Thus, with the eyes of the world
upon her, Morlene unfolded the manuscript and
began its study.

As the document was somewhat voluminous, and
as the issues involved were of such grave import to
the cause of humanity, Morlene decided that she
would proceed about her task with much deliberation.   Had she known the contents of Dorlan's personal letter she would have proceeded with more
dispatch.   This Dorlan knew, and not desiring the
personal element to appear in her study of the plan
enjoined that she should pursue her work without
being influenced by what was contained in his letter.

So, after reading a while, Morlene laid the manuscript aside and spent the remainder of the day in

meditating on what she had read. The second day she did likewise. Morlene began to be much elated, for, as the paper progressed, she saw that Dorlan was treating the subject in a most comprehensive way. Thus, from day to day, she read and pondered, her hopes rising higher and higher.

Sometimes when Dorlan would enter upon the discussion of some particularly difficult question, her old feeling of fear would return, but when in a most masterly manner he would sweep away the seeming difficulties just as though they were so many cobwebs, her heart would leap joyfully. By and by, after the lapse of·many days Morlene drew near to the close of the document. When, on the last day of her perusal, she read the last words of the last page, and her mind flashed back to the beginning and surveyed in general outline the whole, her enthusiasm knew no bounds. In quavering tones the sweet voice of this girl, charged and surcharged with love and patriotism, murmured the words, "Columbia is saved. Let all mankind henceforth honor the name of Dorlan, the hero of humanity." She now secured Dorlan's letter, broke the seal and read as follows, a look of pain deepening on her beautiful face as she read.

THE LETTER.

"DEAR MORLENE:

"As best I could, heaven knows, I have wrestled with the problem assigned to me by you, the queen of my heart. Some one has said that the most *sublime* incident in all of human history was Martin Luther's standing alone before the Diet of Worms. Side by side with that statement let all men now write that my situation is the most excruciatingly *painful* one that a human being has ever been called upon to endure. When I first met you, circumstances forced me to stifle the love that was ready to burst into a flame. Subsequently, fate decreed that you should be free, and my heart ran riot.

"But fate was determined that one so beautiful and so worthy as yourself should not be won until the wooer appeared in some degree worthy of the lady whose hand was desired.

"Now, dear Morlene, tell me by what process, human or divine, I could be made in any measure worthy of you? If this plan is supposed to achieve that result, is supposed to mark me as worthy of your hand, it has failure written on its face. This conclusion would seem to be beyond the realm of debate. And yet my reason tells me that the plan must of necessity succeed; that, being based upon incontrovertible laws there is no way for it to fail.

"Now, Morlene, my darling, with my powers of intuition telling me that I must fail of winning your hand and with my reason telling me I have successfully performed the task assigned me, what must I do? Hope and Fear have come to terms in my bosom, and one occupies the throne one minute and the other the next. They alternate thus by day and by night. In my dreams I am sometimes as happy as the angels are reputed to be—happier than they, I should say. But the joy is short-lived, and in my dreams I find myself tumbling over precipices and wading through miry swamps.

"I could not stay in R——, and in quietness await your verdict. I have had to travel, to lessen, if possible, the strain of anxiety upon my mind. So, when you find yourself reading this letter, I shall be hundreds of miles away at Galveston, Texas, on the beach of the great Gulf. I am here awaiting your verdict. If it is favorable, I shall return to you forthwith. If unfavorable, I am at a port where ships are daily leaving for all parts of the world. Enough for that.

"Finally, dear one, if the scheme which I submitted to you affords the necessary assurance that the problem will be solved, telegraph to me the one word, 'Unfettered.' If it does not afford such assurance, let your message be 'Fettered still.'

"Am I yours,

Forever or Never?

"DORLAN WARTHELL."

When Morlene finished reading the letter it was covered with the tears that had sped down her cheeks. "Dear, dear boy! how much he must have suffered, if he loves me thus!" So saying, she arose and hastened toward the telegraph office for the purpose of sending a message to Dorlan.

"Suppose my delay has begotten in Dorlan the recklessness of despair," thought Morlene, and fear born of the terrible thought seemed to lend her wings.

CHAPTER XXX.

THE TELEGRAM.

Arriving in the city of Galveston, Dorlan, anxious to receive the expected message from Morlene at the earliest possible moment, took up his abode in an establishment just opposite the telegraph office.

Day after day Dorlan took his seat at the window of his room and watched the messenger boys as they hurried to an fro delivering messages. He thought of how much anxiety the countless messages represented, but concluded that his was equal to all the other anxieties combined. Each night, when he regarded the hour as too late to reasonably expect a message from Morlene, he would go down to the beach and gaze out upon the great expanse of waters. The tossing waves and the heaving billows reminded him of his own heart. The tides would roll in to the shore and the waves would lap his feet with their spray, as much as to say, "Come with us. We are like you. We are restless. Come with us." Dorlan would look up at the watching stars and out into the depths of the silent dark. Then he would whisper to the pleading waves: "Not yet. Perhaps some day."

Dorlan's *love*, in keeping with the well earned reputation of that master passion, had led him to hope for an early answer from Morlene, in spite of the extreme gravity and manifold complexity of the question that she was now trying to decide. His *reason* told him better than to expect so early a reply. Thus, when love gave evidence of disappointment, reason would say, "Much love hath made thee mad, my boy. Give the dear girl a chance, will you?" At the close of each day this colloquy between love and reason would take place.

But Morlene's delay began to extend beyond the utmost limits that Dorlan had set. Thereupon love's tone became more insistent and the voice of reason grew correspondingly feeble.

Dorlan at last concluded that Morlene's decision was unfavorable to him, and that she hesitated to deliver the final blow. Every vestige of hope had fled and he now kept up his daily vigil purely out of respect for Morlene, not that he longer expected a favorable answer.

Unwilling for Morlene's sake to listen in the nights' solitude to the wooing of the restless waves, Dorlan changed his nightly course and moved about in the city. As he was listlessly wandering through the city one night, he came upon a crowd standing in a vacant lot listening to a man detail the reputed virtues of medicines which he was trying to sell.

The medicine man's face was handsome, his

head covered with a profusion of flaxen hair which fell in curls over his shoulders. His voice had a pleasing ring and his whole personality was alluring. On the platform with the man was a group of Negro boys who provided entertainment for the crowd in the intervals between the introduction of the various medicines. Dorlan stood on the outer edge of the throng and thought on the spectacle presented.

The white people of the South, as evidenced by their pleasure in Negro minstrelsy, were prone to regard the Negro as a joke. And the unthinking youths were now employed to dance and sing and laugh away the aspirations of a people.

Dorlan's veins began to pulsate with indignation as he reflected on the fact that the ludicrous in the race was the only feature that had free access to the public gaze. He was longing for an opportunity to show to the audience that there was something in the Negro that could make their bosoms thrill with admiration. In a most unexpected manner the opportunity was to come.

The medicine man near the hour of closing addressed the audience, saying : "Gentlemen, it pains me to state that our aeronaut is confined to his bed and will be unable to-night to make his customary balloon ascension and descent in the parachute. That part of our evening' sentertainment must there-

fore be omitted, unless some one of you will vol-
unteer to act in his stead."

The last remark was accompanied with a smile,
the speaker taking it for granted that no one would
be willing to take the risk.

"Two birds with one stone," said Dorlan. "The
boys have taught this audience how to laugh. I
can show them an act of bravery. One bird!

"There must be a great force somewhere directing the affairs of the universe. His plannings puz-
zle me. Men have accidentally gone from balloons
to solve the great mystery of all things. Bird
number two! Morlene evidently does not care."

Elbowing his way through the crowd, Dorlan
clambered upon the platform and said: "Gentlemen, the phases of Negro character are as varied
as those of other men. There is in us the sense of
the humorous and the possibilities of the tragic.
We can partake of life to satiety, we can die of
grief. These boys have made you laugh. Allow
me to awaken in you higher emotions. I will
make the ascension and descent and thus prevent
the marring of our evening's entertainment."

The medicine man looked at Dorlan in astonishment, approached him and talked with him a short
while. Concluding that Dorlan was sane, knew
what he was about, and would not undertake the
feat if incapable of successfully performing it, the
man now had the balloon prepared. The audi-

ence, glad that they were not to be robbed of their expected pleasure, cheered lustily when it was found that Dorlan was to make the trip into the air.

Dorlan stepped into the balloon and was soon being whirled upward. His soul felt a measure of relief as he rose above the staring crowd, above the tall buildings, as he entered the regions of floating clouds, as he passed upward toward the brightly shining moon and the quiet light of the stars. On and on he swept.

The pure air into which he had now come refreshed his spirit and he could look at matters with a clearer vision. "Think," said Dorlan, as he stood in the balloon and gazed into the stellar depths, "how long it took this universe to evolve unto its present state. Think of the seemingly slow process of world formation now going on in the Nebulae scattered through those realms yonder." His mind reverting to his attitude toward Morlene, he said:

"And here I am impatient because that dear girl on whose heart the woes of the world now rest has not hastened in deciding that I had harnessed the forces that will solve one of the most difficult problems that ever perplexed mankind."

The utter unreasonableness of expecting so early an answer upon a question that demanded such earnest thought, now appeared to him as almost

criminal. He saw that the time allowed Morlene, in what he regarded as his saner moods, was
thoroughly inadequate. These moments of elevation and reflection restored hope to his bosom.

Stimulated by the thought that Morlene was not
necessarily lost to him as yet, Dorlan now caused
the balloon to start toward the earth. He would
have liked to come down all the way in the balloon
since he was no longer yearning for death, but he
remembered his brave speech and the expectations
of the crowd below. So, in spite or his keen desire
to live, he decided to maintain his honor in the
eyes of the waiting audience and descend in the
parachute at whatever cost. Not knowing what
would be his fate, Dorlan sprang out of the balloon, trusting to the parachute. At a terrific speed
he shot downward toward the earth. For a few
seconds the parachute seemed that it was not going
to bear him safely to earth, but, happily for the innocent Morlene, soon readjusted itself. Down,
down, down, it came bringing to the murky atmosphere, to the crowded streets, to the regions of jar-
ring ambitions, the troubled spirit that sought in
an hour of despair to fly its ills.

Dorlan reached the ground in safety and received
the congratulations of the spectators, who, guided
by the light attached to the balloon, had succeeded
in locating the possible point of descent.

Dorlan now went home, fully resolved to await
in calmer spirit the expected answer.

One day as Dorlan was sitting before his window, he saw a messenger boy come out of the telegraph office, pause and look up at the number on the house in which he was stopping.

The boy then started across the street in Dorlan's direction. Dorlan ran out of his room and down the steps, reaching the door before the boy. Sure enough the telegram was for Dorlan. He snatched it from the boy and handed him a dollar.

Dorlan turned to go up stairs. " Wait for your change, Mister. We don't get but ten cents extra."

" Keep the dollar, lad," said Dorlan, hurrying up the stairway. Entering his room he gently laid the telegram upon the center table and stood back to gaze upon it. Dorlan could not conceive how he could endure the excess of grief if the message was unfavorable, or the excess of joy if it was favorable. Cautiously he approached the table, then seized the telegram and tore it open.

The next instant the lady of the house verily thought that a Comanche Indian had broken into her establishment, so loud was Dorlan's shout of joy when his eyes fell on the one word, " Unfettered." Her astonishment was even greater when Dorlan so suddenly departed, leaving in her hands a roll of money far in excess of her charges.

Dorlan had no time for explanations. The soul that had come into the world to mate with his was

calling for him and all other considerations had to
fade away.

*　　　　*　　　　*　　　　*　　　.*　　　　*　　　　*

As the train rolled into the shed adjacent to the
great depot at R——, Dorlan, who was standing
on the platform of a coach, caught sight of Morlene, who had come down to the station to meet
him. He seemed to feel that he could cover the
remaining distance between himself and Morlene
quicker than the train, for he leapt upon the platform before the train stopped and urged his way
through the throng to the spot where she
stood.

Then, half forgetting and half remembering the
multitude present, Dorlan grasped the outstretched
hands of Morlene drew her to him, and planted on
her lips a kiss—just one, mark you. The ladies who
were standing near looked searchingly at Dorlan,
and rendered a silent verdict that Morlene could be
excused for not resenting the salutation from so
handsome and so noble looking a man.

The men looked at Morlene and wondered how
Dorlan could be content with just that one. Those
men always thereafter gave Dorlan the credit of
being a man of marvelous self-control. You see,
they did not consult Morlene on that point, who
and who alone knew how frequent and how fervent
were those manifestations of regard after the proper

authorities had said that she was to be Mrs. Morlene Warthell thenceforth until death.

*   *   *   *   *   *   *

Over the hillsides of life, through its many valleys, alongside its babbling brooks, in the splendor
of the noonday, in the gloaming, in deepest shades
of evening, on and on, Dorlan and Morlene go,
happy that they are freed from the narrow and nar-
rowing problems of race; happy that at last they,
in common with the rest of mankind, may labor for
the solution of those larger humanistic problems
that have so long vexed the heart of earth.

We now bid this loving and laboring couple a
fond adieu, well knowing that wherever in this
broad world these true souls may wander they will
be gladly received and housed as the benefactors
of mankind.

THE END OF UNFETTERED.

DORLAN'S PLAN.

(SEQUEL TO "UNFETTERED.")

A DISSERTATION ON THE RACE PROBLEM.

BY

SUTTON E. GRIGGS.

"The solution of the Negro Problem involves the honor or dishonor, the glory or shame, the happiness or misery of the entire American people."—*Frederick Douglass.*

"I had rather see my people render back this question rightly solved than to see them gather all the spoils over which faction has contended since Cataline conspired and Cæsar fought."—*Henry W. Grady.*

FOREWORD.

PRIOR to the coming of Dorlan Warthell, there were many to be found in the United States who utterly despaired of a happy solution of the problem of adjusting the relations of the Anglo-Saxon and Negro races to each other on an honorable and mutually satisfactory basis, taking care the while to meet the highest demands of the present and of all future ages.

Others, while not despairing, confessed that in the horizon subject to their vision not a glimmer of light appeared; confessed that they were only sustained by their general knowledge of nature's power to solve, through tears and years, all her problems.

Thus, until the day when Dorlan came, Columbia sat chained on the one side by benumbing pessimism and on the other by deferred hope. Accepting the judgment of so sweet and true a soul as Morlene, it was he who solved the problem. In view of the complicated nature of the problem and the great interests involved, its solution must ever be regarded as a noteworthy achievement.

It occurred to us that the ages which now sleep in the womb of time would be pleased to ponder the achievement, hoping to find in the spirit and method of its undertaking, suggestions that would enable them to deal wisely with the problems of their day.

For the sake, therefore, of posterity we have concluded to place on record a copy of Dorlan's Plan by means of which he swept away the last barrier that stood between himself and the woman who had entered into his life to give color to the whole of his existence in this world and in such other worlds as may afford a dwelling place for the spirit of man.

Perhaps a majority of those who have read " Unfettered" and have learned to share Dorlan's exalted opinion of Morlene, will not care to read the Plan, being content to rest the whole matter upon Morlene's decision. Those who pay such a tribute to our heroine may thus escape the tedium of wading through the dry details of a plan by means of which a long suffering race was saved.

Others who may be disposed to question Morlene's judgment, who think that her love for Dorlan influenced her to decide in his favor, are hereby furnished with the Plan and ordered to read it as a befitting punishment for their temerity.

As these "doubting Thomases" wearily plod their way through the Plan we hope that they will have ever present with them to add to their torture, the thought that they would have escaped the punishment of reading all that Dorlan wrote had they meekly accepted Morlene's verdict. As wail after wail shall arise proclaiming what dull reading the Plan makes, we shall chuckle gleefully and rub our hands joyfully, happy that those who would not take the word of our heroine have come to the end so richly deserved.

Those who accepted Morlene's verdict and now read the Plan simply for the purpose of defending her from hypercritical personages are heroes indeed. For, be it remembered, it often requires more courage to read some books than it does to fight a battle.

Such may be the case with Dorlan's Plan, and all have fair warning.

THE AUTHOR.

DORLAN'S PLAN.

WHERE THE TROUBLE ARISES.

THE Negro is a human being. He has manifested every essential trait of human nature.

The following words from Emerson, spoken of each individual member of the human family, may be specially affirmed with regard to the Negro : "What Plato has thought he may think; what a saint has felt he may feel; what at any time has befallen any man, he can understand."

The general laws governing the physical and psychic natures of men; that unfold the workings of the human body and the mental, moral, religious, social and æsthetic processes of the soul—the general laws governing these operations may be applied with as much force to the Negro as to any other human being.

This has been an age of astounding discoveries; but the physiologist, the pscychist, the ethical writer, the ecclesiastic, the sociologist, the investigator of æsthetic manifestations, the ethnologist, the philologist, the natural scientist, though searching eagerly, have discovered naught to controvert or in anywise impair the doctrine of the unity of the human race as set forth in the declaration of Paul, "that all nations of men" have been "made of one blood to dwell on all the face of the earth."

Those who concede to the humanity of the Negro and hold to the theory that man is upon the earth through the direct, specific, creative fiat of God, are forced to admit that the Negro's certificate of membership in the human family is signed by the Deity, and by virtue of that fact must be received at face value.

He who holds with the evolutionist that man is the product of evolutionary forces, working incessantly through the countless ages that lie behind us, must perceive that, in that event, the Negro can point to the fact that his presence in the human family has the sanction of the multiplied myriads of experiences that, from one forge, out of one material, through the one process, made him along with other human beings. If God is represented as presiding over the forces of evolution, the Negro may claim that God and nature have fixed his status as a human being.

Being forever established by the Supreme Architect of the universe within the line drawn to encircle humanity to the exclusion of all things else, the Negro is entitled to every right that inheres in the fact of his humanity. He is entitled to all the benefits of the feeling of distinctive fellowship—that feeling which operates to bind ant to ant, bird to bird, and man to man, as apart from other orders of beings. He is entitled to the designation, Brother. The Negro has identically the same right to live as other human beings; the same right as they to tread unfettered any and all of the pathways that destiny has marked out for human feet.

It is this conception of the basic, inherent right of the Negro to share on equal terms with all other human beings all the rights and privileges appertaining to membership in the human family that gives rise to the Race Problem in the United States of America. For, while the claim is passionately cherished by the Negroes and is espoused with varying degrees of warmth by one section of the American whites, it is most vigorously opposed by another.

❧

OUR PROBLEM.

IT is our task to so utilize the forces at our command as to nullify all artificial hindrances to the development of the Negro; to remove from his soul the man-imposed fetters; to so open the way that the man with a black skin shall have his opportunities limited solely by his capacity, as is the case with those not of his color. We are to institute merit as the test of preferment; mind, as the measure of the man. To reverse the standard of measurement, to transfer it from color to culture, is our problem.

The plan to be submitted must take cognizance of all the factors in the situation; must be capable of being operated by the race constituted, environed and conditioned as it is. With this conception of our task we begin our labors.

&

THE INSPIRATION OF THE OPPOSITION.

IT is well in every species of combat for a man to seek to know the exact nature of the opposing force. Knowing this, one understands the better how to gauge his efforts. With this aim in view, we shall make a reconnoitre to discover just what is arrayed against us.

Mr. Herbert Spencer says: "It has come to be a maxim of science that in the causes still at work, are to be identified the causes which, similarly at work during past times, have produced the state of things now existing."

We would expect, therefore, to find the past yet affecting the Negro, and such is indeed the case. From the year 1619 until the close of the civil war, the white people of the South held the Negroes in slavery.

It is the habit of nature to confer upon a man those qualities that the better fit him for his line of work. In order to successfully hold slaves, the Southern man fostered the belief that the Negro's humanity was somehow of a different brand from his own. Having satisfied himself that essential differences existed between himself and the Negro, he was the better prepared to mete out treatment which he would have deemed outrageous if applied to himself by another.

To prevent uprisings on the part of the slaves repressive measures were instituted, and the Southern white man became an adept in the art of controlling others, and his nature became inured to the task. The traits of character acquired in one generation were transmitted to succeeding generations, so that notions of inherent superiority and the belief in the right of repression became ingrained in Southern character.

In confirmation of this conclusion, we again quote from Mr. Herbert Spencer, who says: "The emotional nature prompting the general mode of conduct is derived from ancestors—is a product of all ancestral activities. * * * The governing sentiment is, in short, mainly the accumulated and organized sentiment of the past."

In view of the foregoing, it becomes evident that the repression which the Negro encounters to-day is but the offspring of his repression of yesterday.

STILL IN THE BALANCES.

IN Prof. Giddings' "analysis of the population of the United States according to race, he says that the English temperament is represented by about 33⅓ per cent., the prevailing Irish by about 29 per cent. and the prevailing Scotch by about 19 per cent. The percentage, not of course precise, is, he thinks, indicative of the influence on the American life and character of these racial tendencies."

We are laboring to add the voice of the Negro to this national chorus. The giving of the Negro an opportunity for untrammeled activity in the National Government means that much of an addition to and consequent alteration of our characteristic Americanism.

It is evident that the Negro will bring into the national spirit the influence of his peculiar characteristics. Now this adding to and taking from the national spirit is a most grave matter. Often the characteristic spirit of a people is a sole remaining reliance; is often the only asset that the fluctuations of capricious fortune has not swept away.

The great importance that attaches to the spirit that characterizes a nation is set forth by Napoleon Bonaparte in the following words: "Had I been in 1815 the choice of the English as I was of the French, I might have lost the battle of Waterloo without losing a vote in the legislature or a soldier from my ranks." Allusion is here made to that British tendency to persist in a given course and adhere to the standards of chosen leaders in the midst of circumstances adverse and even appalling. On the soil of England and on many another spot where the Englishman's foot has trod, from the dying embers, yea, the smouldering ashes of defeat, victory has so often sprung as the result of the spirit to which Napoleon Bonaparte paid tribute.

The English speaking race holds woman in high esteem, but she has thus far been denied the right of suffrage because of the uncertainty as to what would be the resultant blend arising from her more active participation in the affairs of State.

Mr. Wm. E. Lecky, in opposing the granting of the right of suffrage to the women of England, gave it as his opinion that the emotional element in politics was already sufficiently great without the addition of the strongly developed emotionalism of woman. The same sentiment of conservatism that operates to cause woman's rejection is, beyond question, a factor in our problem.

The Negro has but lately entered civilization's parlor. He possesses an oriental nature called to service in an occidental civilization. Of remarkably quiescent tendencies he must play a part in a government born of a revolutionary spirit and so devised that revolutions may be effected whenever desired through means of the ballot box.

The remarkable manner in which we have responded to the quickening touch of civilization; the revelation of traits of a sublime nature unparalleled in the world's history (witness the keen sense of honor that led us to care for the helpless wives and children of those who were at the seat of war fighting for our continued enslavement); the successful meeting, where conditions were favorable, of every test that civilization has thus far imposed—these considerations influence us to believe that the grasping of the flagstaff by Negro hands but means that the flag will float the higher and flutter the prouder and diffuse through the earth even greater glory than before our coming.

Before we can take up the full place for which we aspire, we must meet and combat the timorous conservatism that has hitherto impeded our progress.

Thus are the lines of battle drawn. On one field stands the hopeful Negro never to be contented save with a man's place. On the opposing field stands the Southern white man with an inherited nature and cultivated sentiments that render the repression of the Negro a congenial task. To one side stands the representative of civilization at large, hesitating about doing more in our behalf until we have fully cleared our skirts of the suspicion that attaches to a new comer into civilization. With this conception of the influences which we are to combat, we now plan for the momentous struggle.

✸

HE WHO HAS HITHERTO FOLLOWED CALLED UPON TO LEAD.

NAPOLEON has said that men of imagination rule the world. When society is in a transitional state, men of imagination are able through clear comprehension of the forces at work, to project themselves into the new era, and, seeing where the movement tends, place themselves at the head of the procession. Those deficient in this faculty cannot perceive the ultimate goal of the processes forming before their very eyes; and, even when new conditions have come bearing the stamp of immortality, they yet are dreaming of a relapse into old conditions that are gone forever. They are thus unfit for the duties of the new era, being devotees of the past. The ruling of the world is, therefore, left, as Napoleon asserts, to men of imagination.

The present moment is one calling for the exercise of this faculty of the mind on the part of the Negro in the United States. Hitherto the Republican party has been looked upon as the agency which was to solve all his problems. This was a very natural expectation as that party has been the agency by means of which so much tending in that direction has been accomplished.

A political party, aspiring for control of the
Government, may choose a paramount issue, but
one in power labors to take care of all interests
committed to it.   Now that the Republican party
has won a place in the hearts of the American
people, the business interests of the country are
insistent that they be cared for first and foremost
The nation is making an effort to extend its com-
merce into all parts of the earth, and the Republican party is implored to be the agency through
which this is to be accomplished.

In view of the many interests committed to its
care, the Republican party seems disinclined to
make a specialty of the Negro Problem.   While
reaffirming its old time position on that subject, it
does not see its way clear to jeopardize all other
interests for the sake of that one plank of its platform.   While the friendship and moral support of
that party is to be retained, and while Negroes
who sympathize with its economic policies should
abide with it, it is not wise for the race to rely
upon it solely for the proper adjustment of the Race
Problem.

In fact, the hour has come when the race must
take the matter of its salvation into its own hands.
In times past, when the battles of the race were
to be fought, others led and the trusting Negro
followed.   In this new era the Negroes must lead,
must bear the main brunt of the battle.   Thus,

while estranging no friends of the past, and fully appreciating the continued necessity of outside assistance wherever attainable, the foreword our new propaganda shall be Self-Reliance.

Having hitherto been concerned with the task of comprehending and imbibing a civilization which we had no appreciable share in developing, our passivity, quiescence, docility, the readiness to follow others, were the characteristics which we mainly manifested.

Now that we are to cast off the role of a nursling and take our place as co-creators of whatever the future has in store for the human race, a new order of talents must be called into operation and a new mode of procedure adopted.

Fortunately for us we have the incentive of a largely inglorious past to be redeemed, and the light of all of man's past to serve as our guide.

*

REVISITING THE ORIENT.

TO gain our first lesson in the work before us, we transport ourselves over land and sea until, standing in the valley of the Nile, we can pause and gaze upon the pyramids of Egypt, reminders of the day when our ancestral home held aloft the torch of civilization. In those pyramids, we behold that stones of enormous size and weight have been lifted to such distances from the earth as to stagger the imagination and inspire wonder in the hearts of all generations of all races that have seen or heard of the feat unparalleled in ancient or modern times.

Some African genius of the long ago constructed a device, now unknown to earth, whereby the several strengths of individuals could be conjoined and the sum of their strengths thus obtained applied to the task of lifting the ponderous stones. Innumerable hosts would have failed in lifting those pyramidal stones to the positions which they occupy had it not been for the aid of the device that enabled them to work conjointly. From these pyramids, eloquent in their silence, persistent reminders of the departed glory of Africa, let the scattered sons of that soil learn their first great need—Co-operation.

Our initial step must be the creation of a device whereby the several strengths of the millions of Negroes in the world may be harnessed to the huge stone of a world hate, to the end that said stone shall be swung aloft and hurled into the sea, sinking by the force of its own weight into eternal oblivion.

*

CLASPING HANDS.

IN view of the fact that we cannot now point to any organization capable of amassing the full strength of the race, and as the absence of such an organization might be construed to indicate that there is no need for such, we now quote authorities that thoroughly demonstrate the absolute need of co-operative effort.

Prince Kropotkin, the eminent Russian naturalist, in discussing co-operation among lower animals, remarks :

"If we * * * * ask Nature, 'Who are the fittest: those who are continally at war with each other, or those who support one another?' we at once see that those animals which require habits of mutual aid are undoubtedly the fittest. They have more chances to survive, and they attain, in their respective classes, the highest development of intelligence and bodily organization."

Darwin, giving the results of his observation among the lower animals, pays tribute to the spirit of co-operation, when he says: "Those communities (of animals) which included the greatest number of the most sympathetic members would flourish best."

Ascending from the lower animals, we find that co-operation is equally as valuable and necessary for man. In the march of humanity toward an ideal civilization, we find those races in the van which have best acquired the art of co-operating, while the rear is brought up by those peoples in whom the instinct of co-operation is thus far missing or but feebly developed.

Prof. Henry Drummond remarks: "To create units in indefinite quantities and scatter them over the world is not even to take one single step in progress. Before any higher evolution can take place these units must by some means be brought into relation so as not only to act together, but to react upon each other. According to well known biological laws, it is only in combinations, whether of atoms, cells, animals, or human beings that individual units can make any progress, and to create such combinations is in every case the first condition of development. Hence the first commandment of Evolution everywhere is, ' Thou shalt mass, segregate, combine, grow large.' "

A recent writer has expressed the thought that "neither material prosperity, nor happiness, nor physical vigor, nor higher intelligence," constitute the difference between the 'higher' and the 'lower' races, but that "those are higher in which broad social instincts and the habit of co-operation exist."

In whatever direction we turn we find evidence of the universality of this law. The voices of science, history and sociology in unbroken harmony sing to the Negro of the necessity of co-operative effort. We must, therefore, proceed at once to the formation of a racial organization truly representative, and able to present the combined resources of the race to the work before us. When this is done the Race Problem will at once assume an acute phase; for the aggregate wisdom and power of the Negro none can wisely ignore. Especially is it to be borne in mind that an aggregation of the kind indicated is calculated to reveal, to develop, to impart added greatness to men already peculiarly endowed with powers of aggressive leadership. We must, then, add to the equation the enormous impetus to be given to causes by the presence of great spirits arousing and guiding the thoughts and energies of earnest, daring millions.

❧

RENOVATION.

WHEN our great organization has been effected it must proceed to the diligent study of such traits and environing influences as have in the past operated to impair the spirit of co-operation. Locating the weak points, we must proceed to induce in the Negro such mental and moral characteristics, and must so regulate his environments as to insure efficient co-operation for all the future

It is an evident fact that the spirit of jealousy is more prevalent in some individuals than in others. The like may be asserted with regard to races. Among the Negroes there appears to be an inordinate development of this feeling of jealousy, which makes itself felt among the humblest and among the highest.   Success on the part of a Negro would appear to be a standing invitation for the shooting of arrows into his bosom.   While a strict surveillance over leaders is highly commendable, the baneful effects of hypercriticism and jealous intrigues are far reaching.   Our racial organization must tear up by the roots this extraordinary predisposition toward jealousy and plant in its stead the flower of brotherly love.

During our prolonged existence in a state of individualism, each man working for himself and by himself, there was but little to engender in a man the spirit of sacrifice in the interest of the race as an aggregation.   When our racial organization is perfected we must write upon every man's heart the following words, causing each one to feel in his own case: "It is expedient for us, that one man should die for the people."

In the work of further congealing the race, of inducing in it the social instincts so needful for efficient co-operation, we have the aid of the scorching flames of race prejudice which flash in the faces of all Negroes thus driving them closer together.

As the wars of David with surrounding enemies made a nation of the loose aggregation of the twelve tribes of Israel; as the hundred years of fighting with France effected the integration of the people of England; as the war of the Revolution sowed the seed that enabled the American people to form a nation out of the thirteen colonies ; as the compact German empire of to-day is the result of outside pressure; just so is American prejudice producing a oneness of sentiment in the Negroes which inevitably leads toward their acting as a unit in matters affecting their salvation.

Having arranged for our organization, we are now to point out the lines along which it is to labor.

*

WHERE TO BEGIN.

REALIZING that we must at every point demonstrate that we are intrinsically as well as constitutionally entitled to the lofty estate of American citizenship, our racial organization must neglect nothing needful in the fitting of the race for the high destiny unto which it is called.

In the work of preparing the race, first and foremost, attention must be given to character building. Any hopes founded on aught else, are illusive. Character is the bedrock on which we must build. In describing the successful nation, Mr. Lecky gives voice to the following sentiments unto which we must pay utmost heed :

"Its foundation is laid in pure domestic life, in commercial integrity, in a high standard of moral worth and of public spirit, in simple habits, in courage, uprightness, and a certain soundness and moderation of judgment which springs quite as

much from character as from intellect. If you would
form a wise judgment of the future of a nation, observe carefully whether these qualities are increasing
or decaying. Observe especially what qualities
count for most in public life. Is character becoming of greater or less importance? Are the men
who obtain the highest posts in the nation, men of
whom in private life and irrespective of party,
competent judges speak with genuine respect? Are
they of sincere convictions, consistent lives, indis-
putable integrity? * * * Itisbyobserving this
moral current that you can best cast the horoscope
of a nation."

✄

"THERE IS NO PLACE LIKE HOME."

IN the matter of character building, first, attention must be paid to the home. Prof. Henry
Drummond has remarked that "the first great
schoolroom of the human race is the home." He
further remarks that "It is the mature opinion of
every one who has thought upon the history of
the world, that the thing of highest importance
for all times and to all nations is Family Life."

The home life of the Negro has had to encounter
many antagonistic influences. The work of home
building could not progress under the institution
of slavery. The present builders of Negro homes
are, therefore, pioneers, in the work, lacking the

aptitude that would be theirs did they inherit natures that descended from many generations of home builders.

Conditions under freedom, though an improvement on the past, have retarded the proper development of the home life of the Negro. Often the Negro husband, having been accustomed to seeing women labor, has no scruples as to his wife's being a laborer, even when her home is full of children. The Negro woman having been accustomed to work often continues to do so, after her aid is no longer needed to help support the family.

The average home is small and housekeeping duties are not onerous. Not many possess libraries, and reading is not much in vogue. Thus many work in order to keep employed.

In other cases the scale of wages paid to the men is so very low that the woman has to come to the rescue as a wage earner. This calls her from her home and children.

It is often the case in large families that the united savings of the husband and wife are insufficient to take care of the family wants, and consequently the children are sent out to work.

The hours of toil for all classes of laborers are very long, so that families are separated from early morning until after nightfall. So close has been the confinement all the week that Sunday becomes the day for general visiting and pleasure seeking. It is very evident that the home life has but a fighting chance under such conditions. And yet other factors are to be added.

The child being required to support himself early, assumes an air of independence, and parental authority is correspondingly weakened.

The home life of the Negro is also quite largely affected by the peculiar hold which the secret society has upon the race. The thought that he will enter a realm where much wisdom abides operates to draw the Negro to the secret society. Then, too, if he is a member of such a body, he has, in the fact of membership, a passport bearing testimony as to his social standing. Again, the aid furnished by these societies during sickness, and their public displays upon the occasion of the burial of their members are strong attractions for the Negroes of limited means and of little note. The Negro not content with membership in one such organization usually joins as many as his means will permit. The meetings of the societies are numerous and are held at night, necessitating much absence from home on the part of both the father and the mother. The lodge meeting also furnishes an excuse to such husbands as may have other reasons for not spending evenings at home.

The weekly church services are held at night, calling for more time from home. In view of all of which it is apparent that we are weak at the foundation, the family life, and strenuous efforts are needed at this point.

Our organization must employ an army of workers to co-operate with Negro mothers in the work of home building. Christian institutions where Negro boys and girls are being trained must be induced to pay especial attention to the question of the Negro's home. The laborers' working day must be shortened, so that they may have more time at home. The white families must be induced to have earlier suppers, so that those who cook for them may return to their several homes the earlier.

The scale of wages must be increased so that the mother and children may be exempt from the task of bread winning. With an increase in wages and the consequent ability to save a portion of his earnings for the 'rainy day,' the lodge will not be the absolute necessity to the Negro that it now appears to him to be. Under these improved conditions the mother and the father can the better co-operate and make the home what it must be. Our racial organization must bend its energies in the direction to accomplish these results. For one thing it must link its great influence to that of the forces laboring for the improvement of the condition of the toiling masses.

RELIGION A FACTOR.

IN his very brilliant work on "Social Evolution," BenjaminKidd remarks that "there is not that direct connection between social development and high intellectual development which has hitherto been almost universally assumed to exist," and "that the wide interval between the peoples who have attained the highest social development and the lowest, is not mainly the result of a difference in intellectual, but a difference in ethical development."

He further states that the human race "would, in fact, appear to be growing more and more religious, the winning sections being those in which, *caeteris paribus*, this type of character is most fully developed." He is firmly of the opinion that "the evolution which is slowly proceeding in society is not primarily intellectual, but religious in character."

The influence of religion upon a people's life is admittedly so great that any program looking to betterment of their condition must take note of the prevailing religious belief. The Christian religion was ingrafted upon our racial life in the days of slavery. As we were in an abnormal state, it should not occasion surprise if many did not get a normal grasp upon the Christian religion.

In the days of slavery the Negro felt that his lot in this world was a rather hopeless one. No where could he catch a glimmer of hope. To him the earth was without form and void. But his optimistic nature had to be fed, and the glories of the world to come, pictured in the Bible, to him became a living reality. Thenceforth his mind rested not on earth. The death bed, the funeral, the grave, the world to come, received the wealth of his spiritual energies. As a natural result the bearings of religion on this present life were lightly passed over, lethargic conditions ensued and the spirit of wise prevision was in large measure absent. The morbid dwelling of the mind of the Negro on anticipated worlds must be discountenanced; a more rounded view of religion inculcated.

Without entering into sectarianism our racial organization must foster such conceptions of religion as will make its ethical teachings, applicable to life in this world, more prominent. With the home life cared for and proper religious instruction guaranteed, our racial organization will have laid secure foundations.

❧

TO WEAR WELL OUR CROWN.

OUR racial organization must bear in mind that we are struggling for untrammeled freedom in the greatest government that human intellect has ever evolved. Without proper culture we cannot meet the requirements of worthy citizenship. We must pay especial attention to our public schools, and see to it that knowledge shall not be lacking. The value that education will be to the citizen, is admirably outlined by Thomas Jefferson, in the following words used in setting forth the purposes of education.

Education is intended :

1. "To give every citizen the information he needs for the transaction of his own business.

2. "To enable him to calculate for himself, and to express and preserve his ideas, his contracts and accounts in writing.

3. "To improve, by reading, his morals and faculties.

4. "To understand his duties to his neighbors and country, and to discharge with competence the functions confided to him by either.

5. "To know his rights; to exercise with order and justice those he retains; to choose with discretion the fiduciary of those he delegates; and to notice their conduct with diligence, with candor and judgment. And in general to observe with intelligence and faithfulness all the social relations under which he shall be placed."

In order to insure the education of the masses, the following steps must be taken:

1. The Negroes must be stimulated to acquire taxable values to such an extent that the Southern States shall not administer the school funds for the

Negroes with the feeling that they are making a charitable donation to the race.

2. Night schools must be fostered for adults.

3. Money must be provided for the lengthening of the school term.

4. Salaries for teaching must be raised that a high order of talent may be the more easily enlisted.

5. Books must be supplied to the children too poor to buy.

6. Means must be instituted to prevent the too common habit of withdrawing the Negro child from school at so early an age to help support the family. These and such other measures as close scrutiny may from time to time suggest must be employed to make the public school system among the Negroes what it ought to be.

❧

IN THE UPPER REALMS.

IT is not enough to provide elementary training for our people. The great minds of earth choose the devious pathways to be threaded by the wavering feet of humanity. They pass upon what is true and what is false, what is right and what is wrong, what is expedient and what is inexpedient. Tremendous is the influence that has been exerted on human history by the teachings of the great.

Through the training of the intellect the Negroes must develop men capable of interpreting and influencing world movements, men able to adjust the race to any new conditions that may arise. We need men to do for the Negro race what Prof. Henry Drummond sought to do for the Christian religion. In the upper chamber of the house of human knowledge, the congress of scientists presided over by Charles Darwin, and representing the culture of the ages, met to promulgate a new religion; a religion that would establish Nature as our ethical teacher, pointing with the finger of evolution, the way for man to go. By dint of patient, faithful labor and notable achievements in the realm of science, Prof. Drummond secured admittance into this upper chamber and took his seat at the council table. Soon the world heard his voice proclaiming in the tone of one speaking with authority that the new revelations of science contained no poison for Christianity; that the new teacher, Nature, was the friend, not the enemy, of the old teacher, the Bible. He declared that Evolution and Christianity have "the same author, the same end and the same spirit."

Thus Drummond was on hand to seek to stay the Darwinian hand, if, after shattering other conceptions, it had attempted to demolish the one worship that modern civilization has thus far failed to destroy.

To prepare Negroes for taking care of our interests in the realms of highest thought, our racial organization must found universities, liberally endow scholarships, provide equipments for original investigations and so foster the cause of higher education that no race can boast of superior intellectual attainments.

~

"OF MAKING MANY BOOKS THERE IS NO END."

BOOKS are the means by which each successive generation comes into possession of the best (of which the records have been kept) that was wrought during all preceding generations of human endeavor. Not only does the art of printing thus connect with all that was good in the past, but it also affords a man the opportunity of becoming a part of all that is being done in his day.

In view of these considerations it is evident that a race that does not read must ever be a laggard race. Our racial organization must, therefore, found libraries throughout the regions in which Negroes dwell, to the end that we may have the benefit of all the elevating influences of good literature.

Our problem is, however, deeper than the mere founding of libraries, as is apparent from the following considerations: During their sojourn in America the great majority of Negroes have had such work assigned to them as required much bodily exercise. But a comparatively few have led sedentary lives. The laboring Negroes have been accustomed to sing as they worked or have relieved the monotony of their labors by jovial bantering. The occupations of a race eventually make themselves felt in more or less marked racial characteristics.

Thus, when a cotton factory was established recently to be operated by Negro labor, it failed, the manager assigning as a partial cause thereof the fact that the Negroes did not make the best operatives, in that sitting still and being quiet caused them to be rather listless and sleepily inclined. While, in other instances, tendencies in that direction have perhaps been overcome, this one case serves to suggest that the inattention to reading on the part of so many may be traceable to the same inherited indisposition to sit still and be quiet, necessary concomitants of the reading habit.

Our racial organization must not, therefore, feel that its labors are complete when the libraries are founded. Systematic efforts must be put forth to create in our people a thirst for reading so that they may have ears to hear what the past and present are thundering at us.

WE EAT TO LIVE.

HOWEVER brave, brilliant and resourceful a general commanding an army may be, however loyal and enthusiastic are his soldiers, he must inevitably fail if he neglects his commissary department. The cravings of the human stomach must be provided for or there will be no soul left in the emaciated body to aspire for higher things.

In arranging, therefore, for the welfare of the race our racial organization must not neglect the material needs of our people. An advancing army must protect at all hazzards its base of supplies. We now outline a course of action in keeping with this thought.

The man who knows that there is a prejudice against him, owes it to himself to so contrive that he shall be as nearly as possible independent of the workings of this prejudice. Negroes, therefore, should, in the main, seek those callings in which they shall be above the whims and prejudices of men.

The land owner, the farmer, can come as near to being independent of his fellows as a man may in these days attain. The sun, the elements, the soil, his own strong arm, are his chief reliance and these forces are not subject to enslavement, nor can prejudice weaken them. Nature has no favorites among men. The rains fall upon the just and the unjust alike. Back to the farms, therefore, should in a large measure be our cry. With a strong agricultural backbone the position of the race is much the more secure. The conditions that operated to cause the Negroes to so largely abandon the farms must be studied and altered when possible.

Our racial organization shall give due recognition to the following needs, doing all that is necessary to see that they are attained:

1. The Negro must become the owner of the soil he tills.

2. He must be placed above the conditions of dire necessity that causes him to resort to the credit system of buying and the mortgaging of his crops, which things have hitherto wrought his ruin.

3. Provisions must be made whereby he may secure modern appliances with which to farm.

4. He must be educated so that he may know how to obtain the best possible results from the soil.

5. He must be taught to keep fully posted upon the important happenings in the commercial world bearing upon his interests.

6. The Negro must join hands with the students of the agricultural problem in general, ready to avail himself of any new developments of value that may arise.

LITTLE AFRICAS.

IN practically every Southern city there are certain sections inhabited almost exclusively by the poorer, shiftless, more ignorant class of Negroes. The houses in these Negro settlements are small, dilapidated and often situated in marshy regions. The streets or alleys thereof are narrow and crooked and destitute of drainage. In such sections barrooms thrive, gambling dens flourish, and gathering places are afforded for lewd women and vicious men. By day Negro women in filthy, unbecoming attire, barefooted and bareheaded, congregate in the street and engage in loud, unseemly talk. Idle Negro men are to be seen lounging around these settlements. Garbage is emptied into the streets there to remain. Such settlements as these breed disease and are menaces to the health of the cities. They are the places where crimes and criminals of all kinds are developed. They mar the beauty of the cities and keep down the price of real estate in their neighborhoods. They do much to bring the whole Negro race into disrepute. A revolution must be wrought in these settlements at all hazards. The more refined among the Negroes must be employed to labor among the masses and thus ameliorate the ills herein set forth. Tracts of land should be purchased just beyond corporate limits, in easy access to the business centers. Commodious houses should be constructed and sold to the Negroes at moderate prices and on easy terms.

"YE HAVE THE POOR WITH YOU ALWAYS."

THE earnings of the Negroes being small, they have but little opportunity to accumulate a surplus for old age and decrepitude. This evil is accentuated by improvidence. So long as these conditions exist, there must be aged Negroes unable to take care of themselves. For these homes should be established.

Orphan Asylums are sadly needed and must be provided for the tens of thousands of young cast adrift annually through the deaths of impoverished parents. At present youthful Negro offenders are sent to prisons where they are in daily contact with hardened criminals. Reformatories must be established where these beginners in crime may be lured from the paths of vice, instead of being the better educated for evil as at present.

Comparisons unfavorable to the Negro have been so often instituted that the passion for appearing as well or better than the whites has taken hold of many. Living side by side with a wealthy rival race, the Negro often overstrains himself in an endeavor to keep well in sight of the white man. As outgrowths of this condition their church houses, very often, their dwellings, the furnishings for their homes, their dress are wont to cost more than their earnings would warrant. There are money-seeking men who have discovered the depths of this desire of the Negro to appear well.

They have formed loan companies and accept mortgages on all sorts of possessions of the Negroes and exact rates of interest that are astounding.

Dealers in various lines of ware do not hesitate to sell to the Negroes the most costly articles on the installment plan, taking care to place charges thereon far above their real value. Thus the meagre earnings of the race are so largely absorbed in the manner indicated. It means perpetual poverty to the masses unless corrected.

Negroes must be taught to live simply, in keeping with their financial condition. Penny saving banks must everywhere be established, and forces set to work to urge the Negroes to save their money, thus counteracting the influence of the myriad loan offices that tempt them to their financial ruin.

*

THE WINDS HAVE VEERED.

THE age in which we live is fast shifting from a basis in which brute force is a great factor, to one in which skill and intelligence are the prime essentials. The day of the man who has naught to offer save his native strength is fast drawing to a close, and his night is all but upon us.

The general refinement of taste requiring a higher order of intelligence to satisfy it; the in-

ventive genius of man bringing into use complicated machinery—these are influences at work
rendering necessary a greater measure of skill and
a higher order of intelligence in the modern laborer.

If the Negro would not be lost in the shift of
the age, he must be trained with a view to the
requirements of modern civilization.   To this end
Technological schools must be established throughout the South and other centers of Negro labor.

❧

"THE FIELD IS THE WORLD."

THE Negroes have evinced a keen desire for
education, until now there are more educated
young men and women than there is congenial
labor for them.   The schools have sent them forth
far faster than conditions have permitted them to
be absorbed.

The Negro parent that has to submit to great pri-
vations to educate his child, viewing education
from the simple standpoint of its ability to afford a
livelihood, has now under consideration the advisability of continuing his effort to educate his offspring. The pupil, confronted with so many of his
fellows that have gone through school and failed of
congenial employment, is inclined to lay down his
books and bring his school days to a close.   To
relieve this very annoying congestion, Negroes
must invade all the avenues of trade and found en-

terprises that will give employment to the trained members of the race. The labor of the race is fully able to sustain all branches of endeavor incident to civilized life.

Simultaneous with this development of the home field, Puerto Rico, Cuba, Hawaii, the Philippines and Africa must be utilized to relieve this congestion.

The well equipped young men and women must be inoculated with more of the pioneer spirit.

⚜

WHERE THE GALE BLOWS FIERCEST.

IN labor, business, social and religious circles, a citizen is at liberty to avoid contact with an undesirable neighbor if he so elects. As these constitute the bulk of the activities of the American people, the normal relation of the Negroes and whites is a peaceful one. But there are points where contact is unavoidable.

We have a common political structure, common courts and common public utilities. At these points all citizens must meet and such friction as arises comes mainly from these sources. We now outline the program to be carried out by our racial organization at these points, begining with the ballot box.

The United States is pre-eminently a political country, politics occupying a relatively large space in the public mind. With the national thought focused on politics, in that arena a man is more sorely tried, his powers put to more severe tests, his strong and his weak points more clearly developed than in any other sphere of activity. He who emerges from the galling fire of American politics unscathed, must be accorded a crown of unfading glory.

To illustrate the ordeal through which one must pass, we cite the following comment :

" In turning over the files of the American press, we read of Washington as an embezzler ; of Jefferson as an atheist, an anarchist and a libertine ; of Adams as a tyrant ; and of Jackson as a bully, a border ruffian and an assassin. Van Buren was accused of stealing gold spoons from the ' White House.' The stock epithet applied to President Lincoln was the ' Illinois baboon.' President Johnson was habitually described as a ' drunken boor.' What was said by the newspapers of our later Presidents, from General Grant to Mr. Cleveland, is fresh in the memory of every person of mature age. How utterly insincere is all this hideous abuse may be seen in the fact that it is hushed into silence as soon as the object of it passes out of the political arena into private life. No breath of it ever lingers in the allusions that are thereafter made to him by even the bitterest of his late opponents."

The Negro has assuredly received his full measure of blows from the hand of America's master passion. When the Negro stepped into the arena to play his part he had to encounter the feeling of caste, which insisted that he was inherently disqualified to enter, the claim being set up that nature had forever decreed against him in this respect. He was met with violence, with fraud, and vituperation, with misrepresentation, with disregard for all the forms of law. The votes which he sought to cast in his own favor were boldly appropriated to the opposition. His cupidity was tempted, his every weakness exploited. His virtues were minimized and his shortcomings exaggerated and unduly paraded. This treatment of the Negro was not necessarily special. It was in keeping with the rules of American politics in which the Darwinian law of the survival of the fittest everywhere obtains.

In view of the galling fire which all participants in America who enter politics must encounter, our racial organization will be confronted with a serious task in the formulation of the political program for the Negro.

The following suggestions will afford a basis for the projecting of a policy that will enable the race to take care of itself at this, the most crucial, the really pivotal point in its battle for honorable station.

The difficulties in the way must not influence the Negro to regard the political tree as bearing forbidden fruit, as regards himself. Such a course would be an acceptance of the 'class' system, which is contrary to the genius of American institutions.

There is a development that comes from the contemplation of and the participation in the affairs of State. Much of the superiority of the American civilization is due to the fact that its citizens as a body are treated as sovereigns, educated with a view to the fact that they are to pass upon most grave and intricate problems.

Again, as an encouragement to civic virtues the Negro youth, like other youths, must be allowed to feel that the social group which he is expected to serve, is permitted to reward him if his faithfulness to the needs of the group justify such a course. Thus the political door, through which a man enters to receive rewards from the State acting as a body, must never be closed to the Negro. Far be it from the Negroes to ever yield so vital a point. Instead of counselling retirement from politics, our racial organization is to arrange for a wiser participation therein.

The manner of the emancipation of the Negro was most unfortunate indeed. It should have come from the nation as a whole, or should have been the direct result of the Negro's own efforts, if he was to begin his career as a citizen under ideal circumstances. As it is, he has been caused to feel that he owes a debt of gratitude to one party, so great as to constitute a perpetual mortgage. The Negro must shake himself loose from all such feelings if he is to be a true citizen. He must put the nation above the party even if that party is accredited with having done him a personal service. Nor must he be influenced by hatred of the party that in the past was associated with his humiliation.

When our national government was but beginning its career in the family of nations, George Washington warned it against the undue cultivation of love and hatred. Said he in his farewell address :

"Cultivate peace and harmony with all. Nothing is more essential than that permanent, inveterate antipathies against particular nations and passionate attachments for others should be excluded, and that in place of them just and amicable feelings toward all should be cultivated. The nation which indulges toward another an habitual hatred or an habitual fondness is in some degree a slave. It is a slave to its animosity or its affection, either of which is sufficient to lead it astray from its duty and its interest."

He could say this and desire its application to both England and France, though the former had fought against and the latter for the establishment of the republic.

Our racial organization must teach the Negro

to observe this rule with regard to all existing political parties. Let an unbiased study of present and prospective policies influence party affiliations, rather than love and hatred based upon a past forever dead.

It is not wise for the Negroes to aspire to exercise political influence in proportion to mere numbers with a view to securing *race* triumphs. Good government, pure and simple, and not race supremacy, must be the end forever sought. The right to rule must be accorded to the intelligence, to the moral and material worth of every community as ascertained with regard to the whole body of the people, whites and Negroes. No man white or black must be supported or opposed on account of his color.

The ranks of the Negroes must cease to be the place of refuge and the means of power for the renegade weaklings from the camps of the whites, whose only impelling motive is greed for the emoluments of office, and whose only recommendation is the color of the skin. The white face in Negro ranks must cease to bring a premium with the Negroes. That face, like all others, must be adjudged purely upon its merits. The Negroes must convince the better element of Southern whites that they will not take up and honor worthless white men rightfully cast off or denied distinction in and by their own race.

Again, the Negroes must not center their political activities on the mere holding of offices. The office is not always the real seat of political power. In American politics it is sometimes the political boss, sometimes the party caucus, sometimes the committee of the law-making body, that is the actuald etermining factor in matters.

The Negro must make a study of the larger needs of the people and persist in making himself felt at the most effective point. Though not holding office himself he may yet exert a wholesome influence on the man that does, if he but act wisely.

It is said of American politics as a whole, that the best citizens are too largely holding aloof. It is urged that the law making bodies do not any longer represent the highest mental and moral development of the people. Even if the good and strong of other groups of Americans are adopting such a course, the better element of Negroes cannot afford to follow the example.

The interests of the race in matters political must not be left to those least qualified for the responsibilities. Men, good and true, the ablest of the race, must be induced to make the necessary sacrifices and enter politics with a view to taking care at this point of the honor and welfare of the race. Unworthy and incompetent men in the race must be given a back seat, and their influence neutralized in political affairs, the place where we are peculiarly on trial, and where so much may be won or lost.

Finally, knowing that our hereditary influences and environments in the past were not such as were best adapted to preparing a people temperamentally for self-government; knowing that America is infested with a strong color prejudice; knowing that the Negro's own record as a voter and lawmaker is not altogether in his own favor; knowing the difficulties that naturally arise from the attempts to blend such widely divergent race types into a common political life; knowing how galling is the fire upon any one who has the temerity to enter the arena of American politics; knowing these things, the guiding star of the Negro, the light from which his eye must never wander, is Caution. Others with less to lose may " play the game of politics " lightly, but the Negro must give to the task the highest there is in him.

That the policy herein set forth may be carried out; that the Negro may be prepared to demean himself nobly in the maelstrom of American politics, our racial organization shall create a non-partisan bureau that shall thoroughly educate the Negro as to his own history; as to the history of the Anglo-Saxon race; as to our form of government; as to our political parties; as to all the problems confronting our nation; as to the predominating racial instincts of the Anglo-Saxon race which are often in reality more of a governing force with us than mere written laws.

WITH THE HEN GOES HER BROOD.

WITH the adjustment of the political question will come an era of good feeling which will operate to ameliorate other conditions.

The Negro complains that the courts of the South are arrayed against him; that he does not receive there the treatment accorded to other citizens. So much of this as is true is traceable to the fact that the courts are at present sustained by the same race feeling which has for its end the suppression of the Negro.

When the Negro again becomes a political factor and the court is made amenable to Negro public sentiment in common with the rest of the community, care will then be taken that evenhanded justice is meted out to all. Under such conditions the Negroes and white men of the South will be in a frame of mind to meet and join hands for the protection of womanhood, for the suppression of lynching, for the extirpation of criminality in general.

Chief among the reforms to be inaugurated will be the improvement of the very deplorable prison systems, which being operated with a view to producing revenue, are a blot upon our civilization.

When better feelings prevail, the laws regulating public utilities will be such as conform to the desires of the best citizens of all races.

Thus it will be seen how many of the ills that ramified the whole of Southern life were generated from the strife that had its origin at the ballot box.

❧

THE PROBLEM OF THE OTHER MAN.

WITH our racial organization thus laboring to prepare the race to meet the highest requirements of civilization, the subjective phase of the problem is provided for, and we may now direct our attention to extrinsic factors, the forces without, that must be reckoned with.

In the midst of the study of *our* problem, our racial organization must bear in mind the fact that the Southern white man has *his* problem. He is the lineal descendant of the builders of our civilization. We are heirs thereof by adoption; the Southern white man by birth. It must be assumed that the instincts that make possible our civilization are more deeply written in his nature than in that of the Negro. To him primarily, therefore, is committed the task of preserving in the Southland characteristic Americanism. Thus while benefiting by the many noble traits which the Negro brings, the Southern white man must yet resist whatever

Africanizing tendencies that anywhere show themselves. Such is the Southern white man's problem.

There are Negroes that can meet every test of civilization, while there are others upon whom residence in America has wrought but feebly. The Southern white man closes the door in the face of the prepared Negro, holding that to do otherwise would mean the influx of an uncontrollable mass of the unprepared. He also states that coercive methods are necessary to preserve in the South the Anglo-Saxon flavor to our civilization.

The virile elements in all communities are in duty bound to draw the weaker ones up to themselves, but indiscriminate repression and coercion are not the proper means to be employed in these modern times. The weak are to be elevated through the superior forces known to mind and morals.

It is far better for the South and for the nation that the shortcomings of the Negro be conquered by excellencies, than that they should be left as a constantly rising flood tide destined to overleap all walls whatsoever, carrying devastation that many generations will be taxed to repair. The white man of the South must be aided in his work by the people of the whole land. In view of what is required of them, the white people of the South ought, perhaps, to be more highly and more generally educated than those of any other section of the country, whereas the percentage of illiteracy among them is greater than it is in any other section.

Our racial organization must encourage the philanthropists of the world to remember the white people of the South in the distribution of their wealth for benevolent purposes. When education is more general in the South and the white people are conscious that as an aggregation they represent a higher degree of power, they will feel the more inclined to abandon the policy of force, and proceed with the work of intellectually assimilating the Negroes whom they have hitherto thrust out. When thus equipped the good and strong in the South will coalesce and rule by the sheer force of superior worth, which is the only method countenanced by truly civilized peoples.

Recognizing the fact that it is desirable that the Negro be imbued with many of the qualities of the white man, care should be taken that the Negro population be so diffused throughout the country, that no section of the white race shall have more work of this character than it can well perform. Our racial organization shall therefore establish an emigration bureau, that shall drain off unduly congested regions and locate Negroes in more desirable localities. This lightening of the burdens of some places, coupled with the program of more extended education, will aid the Southern white man to do what the world expects of him, namely, preserve his own strong parts and impart strength to, not repress, the weak.

Thus less and less grow the essential elements of the problem as the great bulk- of the Negroes measure up to the standard of the ideal citizen and the Southern white man is the better prepared to shoulder the responsibility that attaches to the post of seniority in the civilization under which we live.

*

OUR LAST FOE.

WHEN all essential factors in the situation have been cancelled our racial organization will find that there remains to be overthrown pride of race, prejudice and self-interest. The Anglo-Saxon race has so long enjoyed the thought of superiority over the Negro, that there will be those to oppose the unfettering of the Negro through the sheer force of race pride. There will be others who will continue in opposition, as a result of prejudice, for which they can assign absolutely no reason. There will still be others who have profited by race antagonisms, who have come into place and power by their ability to crush out Negro aspirations. An era of peace would rob this class of an occupation, and self-interest will influence them to oppose the untrammeling of the Negro.

Against pride of race, prejudice and selfishness, then, our racial organization will find itself pitted in the last instance.

Here, again, we are face to face with a situation that calls for somewhat of a change of front on the part of the Negro. In the days of slavery the Negro who sought for freedom fixed his eye upon the "North Star" and journeyed thitherward. When freedom at last came to the Negro in the South it came from Northern climes His mind has grown accustomed to looking to forces external to the South to bring him his desires.

Enlightened communities are in great measure self-governing, and too much reliance must not be placed on foreign forces. The Negro must more largely seek to utilize forces present in the Southland. There are broadminded men there that are able to rise above all considerations of pride, prejudice and selfishness, and deal with all men according to the mandates of the Golden Rule.

Our racial organization must form an alliance with such white neighbors—must labor with them in matters looking to the highest interests of our common country. As evidence that there is a possibility of such an alliance, we quote the following from "The Washington Post," a leading newspaper in the nation's capital, and a recognized champion of Southern interests : "So far as we are concerned—and we believe that the best element of the South in every State will sustain our proposition—we hold that, as between the ignorant of the two races, the Negroes are preferable.   They

are conservative ; they are good citizens ; they take
no stock in social schisms and vagaries ; they do
not consort with anarchists; they cannot be made
the tools and agents of incendiaries. * * *
Their influence in government would be infinitely
more wholesome than the influence of the white
sansculotte, the riffraff, the idlers, the rowdies,
and the outlaws."

MIGHTIER THAN THE SWORD.

WHILE paying strict attention to our home influences, we must not be unmindful of the outside world.   If we can bring to bear upon the local
situation the moral support of other sections of our
country and of other civilized lands, our travel in
the direction sought will be the faster.   One of the
chief labors of our racial organization will be to
lay the case of the Negro upon the heart of the
world and cause all humanity to lift a voice in our
behalf.   As evidence that this course is pregnant
with hope, we cite the following authorities :

Herbert Spencer designates " the control exercised by public sentiment over conduct at large"
as " irresistible." He further says: " It requires
only to contemplate the social code which regulates
life, down even to the color of an evening necktie,
and to note how those who dare not break this
code have no hesitation in smuggling, to see that

an unwritten law enforced by opinion, is more peremptory than a written law not so enforced. And still more on observing that men disregard the just claims of creditors, who for goods given cannot get the money, while they are anxious to discharge so-called debts of honor to those who have rendered neither goods nor services, we are shown that the control of prevailing sentiment, unenforced by law and religion, may be more potent than law and religion together, when they are backed by sentiment less strongly manifested. Looking at the total activities of men, we are obliged to admit, that they are still, as they were at the outset, guided by the aggregate feeling, past and present."

Huxley remarks : "It is only needful to look around us to see that the greatest restrainers of the anti-social tendencies of men is fear, not of the law,. but of the opinions of their fellows. The conventions of honor bind men who break legal, moral and religious bonds; and while people endure the extremity of pain rather than part with life, shame drives the weakest to suicide."

Moses, recognizing the influence of the crowd even when in the wrong, felt the necessity of imbedding in the Jewish code this declaration: "Thou shalt not follow a multitude to do evil."

Jesus Christ in projecting a world-wide kingdom designates public reprobation as the highest form of punishment to be known in his realm. "Let him be unto thee as an heathen man and a publican."

The exponents in the Anglo-Saxon race, of justice, liberty, equality and progress, have contended most zealously for the freedom of the press and have evinced in every way a keen appreciation of the value of this instrumentality developed among them for the utilization of the force of public sentiment. In discussing the manner of effecting results in problems of the general nature of ours, Benjamin Kidd remarks: " * * * * In like manner the effect produced on the minds of the British people by descriptions of the wrongs and sufferings of oppressed nationalities, has been one of the most powerful influences affecting the foreign policy of England throughout the nineteenth century; and any close student of our politics during this period would have to note that this influence, so far as the will of the people found expression through the government in power, has been a far more potent factor in shaping that policy than any clear conception of those far reaching political motives so often attributed to the British nation by other countries."

Resolved upon the enlistment of the enlightened sentiment of the world, our racial organization must utilize the talent of the race for oratory and send able men with burning hearts to speak with flaming tongues of such wrongs as the South wittingly or unwittingly imposes upon us. Negro newspapers must be supported, until their unquestioned excellence makes a way for them into homes without regard to race. Daily newspapers and magazines, favorable to the highest interests of the race, must be established so that the outpourings of the souls of Negro writers may have better opportunities of reaching the world. The poem, the novel, the drama must be pressed into service. The painter, the sculptor, the musical composer must plead our cause in the world of æsthetics. The bird that would live must thrill the huntsman with its song. With the sympathies of the world thus enkindled, there are none who would wish to withhold our rights. Even a Cain cries out against a situation in which every man's hand would be against him. Our racial organization must gird itself for the stupendous task of thus winning our great battle, of thus inducing the iron hand to relax its grasp.

&

THE END DRAWETH NIGH.

SUCH is the program of endeavor to be set before our great racial organization. Local organizations modeled after it, having in view similar aims will be created and put in operation. It is evident that the task before us involves the expenditure of enormous sums of money. It is true that the organization once in operation would be cheerfully and adequately supported by the Negroes. But the placing of it upon such a basis as will disclose its value and secure devotion will require great sums of money.

It so happens that Africa has but recently bestowed upon me, Dorlan Warthell, untold millions. I have no qualms of conscience in thus applying to the Negroes of America funds derived from Africa, for I firmly believe with Mr. Wm. T. Stead in the Americanization of the globe, and believe that in due time the Negroes of America are to be the immediate agents of the Americanization of Africa. Money spent in the uplift of the American Negro is, therefore, an investment in the interests of Africa that will pay a glorious dividend. Once established our organization shall win such a hold on the hearts of the Negroes of the world that the poor and the rich will give unstintedly for its maintenance. The philanthropists within the race may be confidently relied upon to do all that may be justly expected of them in the matter.

It only remains for me to state that I have, after a most careful search, selected the men whose names you find appended. They constitute a provisional congress that will superintend the formation of our permanent organization. The men chosen are noted for their intellectual acumen, broad grasp of affairs, judicial temperament, constructive ability, moral probity, and their capacity for sustained endeavor. Such are the qualities that are *known* to characterize the men who have been chosen to groom this infant race to march as one man to the drum beat of fate.

As I view the matter, here lies before the Negro a field of endeavor as great as the earth affords. He is provided with a sphere of possible activity wherein may be won on American soil, as glorious a crown as was ever woven for human brow.

Equipped with an organization that can amass the full strength of the race; blessed with the presence of great minds now furnished with facilities for the attainment of great ends; cheered by a consciousness of power; aided by the moral effect which our racial unity and our insistent attitude in the right will produce; moving forward unfalteringly in the direction of all that is true and good, decisive results must surely follow.

Thanks to this plan, Morlene, I can now assure you that the death knell of the Negro's night has been rung, the stars have shrunk bashfully out of sight, and happy fingers are even now painting the eastern sky a golden hue, a sure sign that the dawn is here.

Yours humbly,

DORLAN WARTHELL.

THE END.